Basic Aerobatics

Basic Aerobatics

R.D. Campbell and B. Tempest

Airlife

England

This edition published 1989
by Airlife Publishing Ltd
Reprinted 1995

First published in Great Britain by
Granada Publishing 1984

ISBN 1 85310 108 7

Printed in England by Livesey Ltd, Shrewsbury.

Airlife Publishing Ltd

101 Longden Road, Shrewsbury SY3 9EB, England

Contents

Acknowledgements

The authors wish to express their appreciation to the Civil Aviation Authority, Slingsby Engineering Ltd, Air Associates Ltd, British Aerospace, Scottish Division and the Cessna Aircraft Company for the reproduction of certain material relating to UK Legislation and the Slingsby, Fuji, Beagle Pup and Cessna Aerobat aircraft.

Grateful thanks are also tendered to all those persons whose advice and suggestions have been incorporated in this training manual.

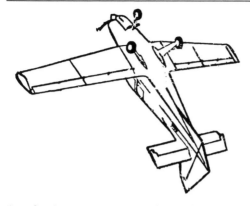

Introduction

Aerobatics manoeuvres have been part of powered flight from the earliest times. Pioneers such as Pegoud, Grahame White, Beachey and Nesterov discovered, probably by accident, figures such as the loop, outside loop and vertical S well before the First World War and included them as features of their Air Show demonstrations. The grimmer needs of air combat in the First World War saw the Immelman turn, snap roll and spin evolve both as a means of attack and evasion. In the period between the wars surplus aircraft and ex-service pilots scratched a living from barn-storming and air circus activities on both sides of the Atlantic with aerobatics attracting the crowds who were then enticed into joy-rides.

Towards the end of the 1930s the first steps were taken towards competitive aerobatics as a sport. In Germany the Jungmeister was designed as a possible standard aircraft for the ill-fated 1940 Olympics when it was intended to initiate aerobatics as an international event.

Once again war intervened and apart from individual pilots enjoying the challenge and satisfaction of aerobatic manoeuvres the main development was the vast expansion of flight training in the combatant nations. Aerobatics were quickly recognised as having enormous benefit in teaching a student to obtain the maximum performance from the aircraft while requiring smoothness and co-ordination. The Tiger Moth, Jungmann and Stearman trainers, while not ideal aerobatic aircraft, demanded a high standard of application to achieve a degree of success. At the same time they were all quite tolerant of aeronautical abuse.

After the war the resumption of competitive aerobatics was slow until in 1955 the Lockheed Brake Company division of Automotive Products, an English company, offered a trophy for annual inter-national competition. This was held at Coventry until 1963 and then at Sywell until the final contest in 1965. Teams and individual pilots mainly from Europe, but also from North and South America assembled each year and the art of competitive aerobatics rapidly progressed. Pilots such as Boddington, Bezak, Price, Ruesch, Aresti and especially Biancotto flew in friendly competition and international aerobatics were a reality.

The Spanish pilot Colonel J. Aresti developed his system of aerobatic manoeuvres notation and classification which was soon adopted on a world wide basis by C.I.V.A., the branch of the F.A.I. responsible for sport aerobatics.

In 1960 the first World Aerobatic Championships were held in Czechoslovakia and these continue on a biannual basis in many European countries and the USA.

On the British domestic scene the patron of light aircraft aerobatics was Norman Jones who founded the Tiger Club in 1957. For the first time an ordinary club pilot could rent an aerobatic aircraft with inverted fuel system. In the 1950s the flying clubs were still largely equipped with war-surplus Tiger Moths and Magisters with basic aerobatic capabilities, however, these were outclassed by the Stampe, Zlin and Yak aircraft flown by foreign competitors. Events such as the Esso Tiger Trophy were instigated and pilots like Peter Phillips, Neil Williams, and Elwyn McAully came to be reckoned with as formidable competitors on the international stage.

Exchange control restrictions on the import of aircraft caused an enormous change in the type of aviation throughout Western Europe in the 1960s. The popular American types were largely non-aerobatic and the sport was kept alive at club level by the rare enthusiastic instructor who was required by the system to be proficient in the art of teaching and performing the basic aerobatic manoeuvres. Eventually however, the Cessna Aerobat development was imported and this type now represents the most common aerobatic aircraft on the British Register. Several other aerobatic trainers in smaller numbers are now available on the club scene.

In more recent years the requirement that all instructors be assessed and trained in their aerobatic skills has been relaxed. Now only instructor examiners must hold aerobatic instructor privileges. Other instructors can, if they desire, take a specific course to enable them to remove the aerobatic instruction restriction on their ratings.

The representative body responsible to the Royal Aero Club for competitive aerobatics in the UK, is the British Aerobatic Association, formed in 1973. They organise regular events through the spring, summer and early autumn at Standard, Intermediate, Advanced and Unlimited level leading to a points Championship at each grade.

Aerobatics provide for the PPL an exhilarating new facet of aviation. It is a constant challenge at every phase and certainly offers a far more effective way of achieving personal satisfaction than most other aviation activities. Application and perseverance are probably the most important areas of effort by the student, backed up of course by a competent aerobatic instructor to advise and encourage the student in his struggle for perfection. Responsibly approached aerobatics form an extremely safe sport, however, height is insurance. Respect for aircraft limitations and the knowledge of your own personal limits are essential. Perhaps the Tiger Club cockpit panel notice sums it all up – 'All aircraft bite fools'.

DISPLAY AEROBATICS

At air displays one may well see aerobatics performed at low height by well known aerobatic pilots. These individuals are, in the main, professionals in every sense having devoted considerable time and money to develop spectacular aerobatic demonstrations. Nevertheless a significant number of fatalities have occurred over the years during low level aerobatic practice and displays, hence the need for the inexperienced to conduct these manoeuvres at a safe altitude.

The Civil Aviation Authority General Aviation Branch is responsible for issuing permissions and exemptions from the Air Navigation Order in respect of the vast majority of air displays. This Branch recognises the British Aerobatic Association Air Display Performers certification and the Historic Aircraft Association's pilot registration schemes as being an indication of the level of skill held by individual display pilots. The addresses of these two Associations are as follows:

British Aerobatic Association Ltd
50a Cambridge Street London SW1V 4QQ

The Historic Aircraft Association
Professional Registers
Registration Secretary
c/o Test Pilot's Office, British Aerospace, Aircraft Group,
Hatfield, Herts AL10 9TL
Telephone 07072 62345

A major benefit of membership of the foregoing Associations is that you may obtain advice and assistance in the vital early stages where experienced display pilots may help you avoid the risks inherent in this form of aerobatics. Frankly there is no place for the irresponsible extrovert among the small fraternity of aerobatic display professionals.

Guidelines for safety arrangements at flying displays are available and published in the CAP 403 by the CAA, and for those pilots who might be interested in taking their aerobatic skills beyond the basic stage we have included the following extracts from the British Aerobatic Association's introductory leaflet.

British Aerobatic Association Ltd
50a Cambridge Street London SW1V 4QQ

AN INTRODUCTION TO COMPETITION AEROBATICS

WHY AEROBATICS?

Briefly, aerobatic training develops a pilot's flying skills to the ultimate. It demands a high degree of dedication and an investment in terms of time and, at the higher levels, money. But in return it provides not only pleasure but also a real mastery of the art of flying in every attitude of flight and in every condition that can be encountered in an aeroplane. Perfecting one's aerobatic skills will inevitably lead to greater self-assurance in handling the machine and greater safety in the air. And there is enormous satisfaction, too, in the precision and artistry involved.

THE BRITISH AEROBATIC ASSOCIATION

We hope the following information will encourage the interest of pilots, non-pilots, prospective contestants and non-contestants alike. The BAeA has the responsibility of promoting and organising all aspects of competition aerobatics in the UK including training, proper conduct and furtherance of the sport, and of course arranging the contests. It is comprised entirely of enthusiastic volunteers (it goes without saying that they are all amateurs!) of whom about 50% are contestants and 50% are supporters. Subsidies are non-existent, so these people's modest subscriptions are all the financial means available to the Association for its normal run of events. Associate Membership presently costs £6 and its benefits include regular information on UK and world-wide aerobatic activities via the six bi-monthly Newsletters. Pilot contestants take out Full Membership at £15 per annum.

HOW IT ALL STARTS

Pilots with basic aerobatic training on, for example, the club Cessna 150/2 Aerobat may well reach the stage of wishing to test their skills in competition with others. Experience may be gained in the annual Cessna Aerobat Contest held by Leicester Aero Club, or the de Havilland Moth Club contests or Tiger Club events, or indeed in local flying club competitions. Sooner or later, having dipped an exploratory toe in at the shallow end, a few of them will be spurred on to arrange some rather more intensive training in order to equip themselves for a BAeA competition. New contestants will start at the Standard Level of competition (of which there are at least three in the season) and this is when they submit themselves to the rather more stringent standards of accuracy, positioning and presentation that are required when competing in earnest. There are then three higher levels to which a pilot may aspire – Intermediate, Advanced and Unlimited – but the Standard Level competitions are always the most well-attended and light-hearted and attract a wide variety of aircraft types: among them the Stampe, Chipmunk, Tiger Moth, CAP10B, Tipsy Nipper and Cessna Aerobat.

HIGHER AND HIGHER...
Moving on to Intermediate and Advanced levels demands an aeroplane with an inverted fuel system, and here the Zlin, Pitts, CAP and other specialised aerobatic types come into their own. The programmes flown during competitions may include any combination of four short sequences:

(1) the BAeA compulsory sequence for that season;
(2) the pilot's own compilation of manoeuvres from the Aresti Dictionary;
(3) a previously unseen and unrehearsed sequence performed on the day;
(4) a totally free non-Aresti sequence composed by the pilot with a time limit of (usually) 4 minutes.

Once into the Advanced and Unlimited league, pilots will be up for team selections to represent the UK at European and World Championships, as well as competing as individuals in the many international events every year. There are internationally accepted standards of excellence and criteria of judging, determined by the governing body C.I.V.A., and all National, European and World Championship Competitions are held in accordance with C.I.V.A. rules. Normally there is either a World or European Championship each alternate year; and Britain will be the host country to the World Aerobatic Championships of 1986.

SUPPORT BRITISH AEROBATICS
In any capacity, in the air or on the ground, the more involved you are the more enjoyable it is. If you would like to make a contribution to the sport and learn more about it – attend aerobatic contests as a helper or spectator – above all, join as an Associate Member of the BAeA. We need your support, and you can make a big difference. If you are a member of a club or similar group, perhaps you might prefer Corporate Membership.

Details of the Association, the various types of membership, and application forms are all available from the British Aerobatic Associaton at the address shown. You can also get T-shirts, caps, stickers and other memorabilia: and you can be sure that all subscriptions and proceeds will play a vital part in helping to perpetuate the tradition of British involvement at the forefront of this sport.

Technical Subjects

Technical Subjects

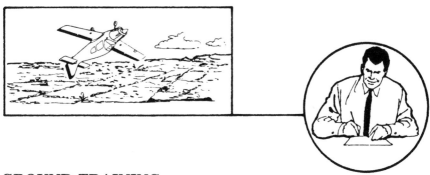

GROUND TRAINING

INTRODUCTION

Much of the information contained in this section will already have been touched upon at some stage during your initial pilot training. However no manual written to assist you to develop aerobatic competence can ignore the importance of revising certain items of knowledge, for example, because of the stresses and strains which a pilot can impose on an aircraft during aerobatic manoeuvres it is essential that you have more than an elementary grasp of how these stresses occur and appreciate to the full the need for remaining within the aircraft's structural limitations as well as your own at all times.

Additionally you will need to understand that not all aircraft cleared for aerobatics are built to withstand the same load factors. Therefore the contents of the following pages should be studied carefully and you should not hesitate to discuss with your instructor any queries which might arise from reading the contents of this section.

LEGISLATION AFFECTING AEROBATICS AND DISPLAY FLYING

Although the legislative documents rarely refer to aerobatic flight specifically, it must be appreciated that unless special exemptions are applied for, and granted by the CAA, a pilot will have to abide by all the current regulations as applicable to the type of flight as shown in the Air Navigation Order, the Air Navigation (General) Regulations and the Rules of the Air and Air Traffic Control Regulations. In addition a pilot should abide by the information regarding aerobatic manoeuvres and Display Flying as contained in the Civil Air Publication No. 403.

Pilots who intend to carry out flights involving aerobatic manoeuvres should, in particular, bear in mind the contents of Articles 45 and 46 of the ANO, and Rule 18 of the Rules of the Air and Air Traffic Control Regulations which are reprinted below:

Article 45 – *Imperilling safety of aircraft.*
> A person shall not recklessly or negligently act in a manner likely to endanger any aircraft, or any person therein.

Article 46 – *Imperilling safety of any person or property.*
> A person shall not recklessly or negligently cause or permit an aircraft to endanger any person or property.

Rule 18 – *Aerobatic Manoeuvres.*
> An aircraft shalll not carry out any aerobatic manoeuvre:
> (a) over the congested area of any city, town or settlement; or
> (b) within controlled airspace except with the consent of the appropriate air traffic control unit.

Additionally, all pilots are reminded of the contents of Article 87 and Schedule 13 of the ANO. These specify the penalties which can be incurred and it would be advisable for pilots to bear the contents of these in mind during any flight.

AIRFRAME LIMITATIONS

The strength of the airframe is based upon the weight that it has been designed to carry and the anticipated aerodynamic loads that may reasonably be imposed upon it during flight. Apart from the need for the combined weights of the crew, passengers, baggage, fuel, etc., to remain within the limits specified in the aircraft manual, consideration must also be given to those more complex aerodynamic loadings which are imposed on specific areas of the airframe during the pilot's operation of the control surfaces and changes in the atmospheric conditions, e.g. turbulence.

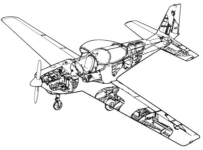

Therefore the loads applied to the airframe can be considered under two separate headings:

(1) the weight being carried by the aircraft together with the position of the centre of gravity.

(2) The aerodynamic loads applied by the pilot and/or the related weather conditions.

THE WEIGHT AND CENTRE OF GRAVITY

The calculation of the weight and its distribution relative to the centre of gravity limitations is a simple mathematical exercise, but it has to be appreciated that in many aircraft which are cleared for aerobatics the weight and centre of gravity limitations will vary dependent upon the category of operation for which the aircraft is about to be used, e.g. touring, training or aerobatic flight. The word 'category' in this context is used to indicate the type of manoeuvres which can be carried out during the particular flight. Its meaning in this case is quite different from the definition of 'Category' in the Air Navigation Order which applies to the purposes for which the aircraft can be used, such as Transport, Private, Aerial Work, etc.

It is also important to appreciate that the terminology used to define whether certain manoeuvres are permitted varies in different countries. In the UK the terminology as laid down in the British Civil Airworthiness Requirements is Aerobatic, Semi-Aerobatic and Non-Aerobatic. Many countries, including the USA and some countries on the continent of Europe use the terms Aerobatic, Utility and Normal. These terms do not necessarily relate to each other in an identical fashion. For example in relation to the term Aerobatic Category the UK also uses the term Semi-Aerobatic and this means that only certain standard aerobatic manoeuvres are permitted and usually excludes such manoeuvres as 'flicks' inverted flight and outside looping manoeuvres.

In order to widen the operational use of some aircraft, the designer may arrange to have the aircraft certificated in several categories, e.g. Normal and Utility, or even Normal, Utility and Aerobatic. In the Normal category the aircraft will be permitted to carry the maximum design load but this weight will have to be reduced when operations are conducted in the Utility category and further reduced if aerobatics are to be performed. In either case the centre of gravity limits will also be restricted.

In view of these variations to the operational category of the aircraft, it will be necessary for weight and balance calculations to be carried out prior to flight. An example of how the particular category is determined for the Fuji FA-200-160, a typical aircraft which could be used in the Normal Utility or Aerobatic category, is shown in Tables 1 and 2.

Table 1   Section 2 Limitations

Category	Maximum Take-off Weight	
	for 7656 propeller	for 7662 propeller
Normal	2335 lb	2270 lb
Utility	2137 lb	2137 lb
Aerobatic	1940 lb	1940 lb

Table 2   C.G. Range

Category	Fwd limit	Aft limit	Weight	Note
Normal (for 7656 propeller)	98.19 (27.0% MAC)	103.58 (36.0% MAC)	2335 lb	Straight line variation between points given
	93.07 (18.5% MAC)	103.58 (36.0% MAC)	1960 lb or less	
Normal (for 7662 propeller)	97.20 (25.3% MAC)	103.58 (36.0% MAC)	2270 lb	
	93.07 (18.5% MAC)	103.58 (36.0% MAC)	1960 lb or less	"
Utility	95.47 (22.5% MAC)	101.77 (33.0% MAC)	2137	
	93.07 (18.5% MAC)	101.77 (33.0% MAC)	1960 lb or less	"
Aerobatic	93.07 (18.5% MAC)	97.58 (26.0% MAC)	1940 lb or less	"

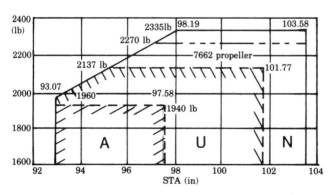

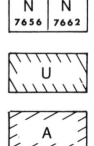

FUJI FA-200-160

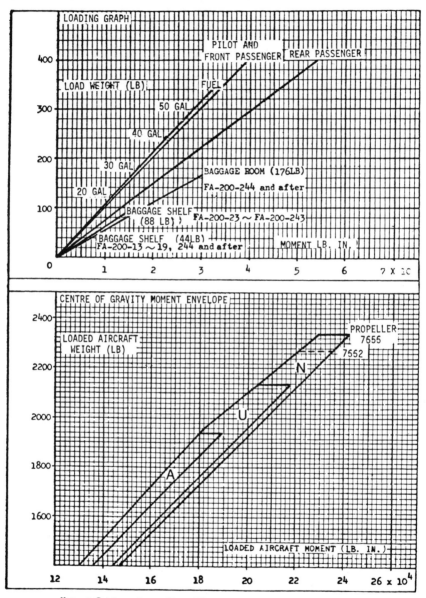

Note : Center of gravity will move rearward with consuming
of fuel, when the calculated C.G position is STA94.2
(20.4% MAC) or after.

Therefore before commencing to carry out aerobatic manoeuvres you will need to ensure that the 'all up weight' and the position of the centre of gravity are both within the aerobatic limits specified for the particular aircraft.

LOAD FACTOR

Having dealt with the question of aircraft weight and centre of gravity, the subject of load factors and how they affect the aircraft during flight can be reviewed. Firstly, load factor should not be confused with 'wing loading'. This latter term is used to describe the relationship between the aircraft's weight and its wing area. It is measured in terms of pounds per square foot or kilograms per square metre. For example an aircraft which weighs 2000 lbs and has a wing area of 200 square feet will have a wing loading of 10 lbs per sq ft, and this will only alter if the weight of the aircraft is changed.

The load factor is the load on the airframe which can be varied by the pilot during flight manoeuvres. To explain this it must be first recalled that the vertical component of the lift force must be equal to the aircraft's weight if it is to remain in level flight i.e. without any change in vertical direction. When this condition is met the value of the load factor is described as 1 (Fig. 1).

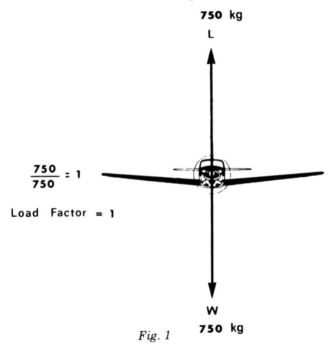

Fig. 1

However if the aircraft is now placed in a turn the lift will be at an angle to the vertical and will be insufficient to balance the weight, therefore the aircraft will descend. If the pilot wishes to remain at a constant level it will be seen that the lift will need to be increased so that its vertical component remains equal to the weight. In the case of a 60° banked level turn the total lift will have to be doubled to achieve this balance between lift and weight and so maintain the aircraft at a constant level. Figure 2 shows this and it can be seen that the lift is now twice the value of the aircraft's weight so the load factor has been increased to 2, which is equivalent to doubling the weight of the aircraft which will increase the stresses imposed upon the airframe.

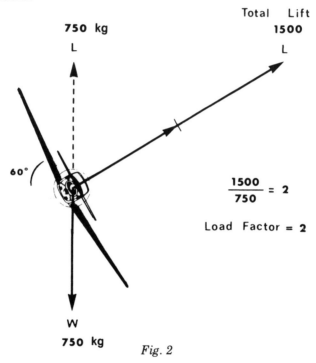

Fig. 2

From this it can be seen that during any turn in which the aircraft remains at a constant altitude the load factor will vary with the amount of bank applied by the pilot.

Figure 3 shows the approximate figures for the load factor as related to bank angle, and it should be particularly noted that the load factor increases very considerably for small increases in bank angle above 70°, a fact which clearly illustrates the need for care during manoeuvres involving large and sustained angles of bank.

So far, load factors have only been discussed in relation to turning flight, however they also apply to other flight manoeuvres involving 'pull ups' or 'push downs' when the aircraft is flying with its wings laterally level. To understand this, the effect of large changes in the

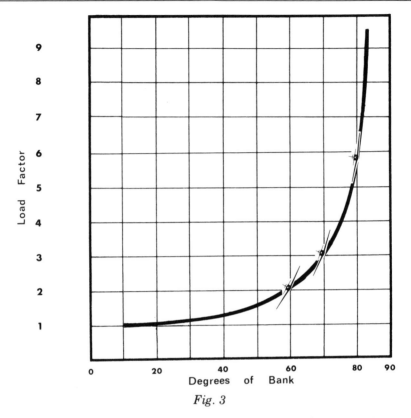

Fig. 3

angle of attack must be considered. For example, assuming an aircraft weighing 750 kg is flying level, in order to maintain level flight at any airspeed the angle of attack used must produce 750 kg of lift as shown in Fig. 4.

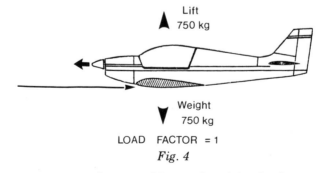

LOAD FACTOR = 1

Fig. 4

If the pilot now applies a sudden and positive back pressure to the control column, the aircraft's attitude in pitch will also suddenly increase. However inertia will prevent the aircraft from immediately changing its flight path and during this period the wings will be presented to the airflow at a large angle of attack, thus causing a large increase in lift. If this momentary increase in lift raised the total lift to 1500 kg then a load factor of 2 would have been experienced by the airframe (Fig. 5). A similar situation could exist if the aircraft flew through a strong vertical gust in the atmosphere. If at this moment a relatively large load factor was being applied, due to control action on the part of the pilot, the additional effect of an increase in the angle of attack as a result of the gust could cause the limiting load factor to be exceeded (Fig. 6).

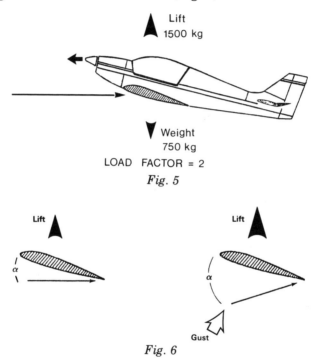

Fig. 5

Fig. 6

Another important influence upon load factor is the indicated airspeed. Although speed does not in itself affect load factor, it does have a pronounced effect on how much of an increase in load factor can be produced by strong vertical gusts, or by sudden and large movements of the controls (primarily the elevators). Because control surface effectiveness is increased with increasing airspeed it becomes easier for a pilot to overstress the aircraft as the airspeed is increased. At lower airspeeds however, sudden and large control deflections will cause the aircraft to stall before a large load factor can be imposed.

The best way to explain these two aspects is to study Fig. 7 which shows the operating strength limitations of an aeroplane presented in the form of a V_n (or V_g) diagram. This illustration does not represent

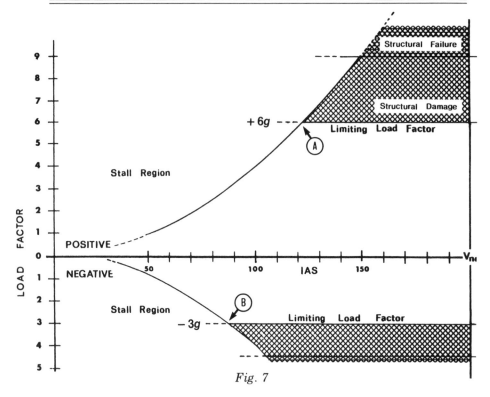

Fig. 7

any specific aerobatic aeroplane but it shows the most important features in relation to structural limitations and load factor. It will be seen that the operating limitations are shown in the form of a graph in which the airspeed 'V' is represented by a horizontal scale and the load factor 'n' is illustrated by a vertical scale. In this presentation the strength of the aircraft is contingent upon four items.

(1) The all up weight of the aircraft.
(2) The configuration of the aircraft, e.g. clean or with flaps, etc., down.
(3) The symmetry of the loading. (The symmetry of loading is important because when asymmetric load factors are applied, i.e. manoeuvring in the rolling and pitching plane at the same time, such as a 'rolling pull out' from a manoeuvre, the structural strength limitations are reduced by approximately one-third.)
(4) The altitude, e.g. density effects.

Item (4) will not be considered in the following paragraphs because it is not particularly applicable to small aerobatic aircraft which operate in the lower levels of the atmosphere.

In Fig. 7 the limiting positive load factor is 6g and the limiting negative load factor is 3g. However to provide for any rare instance when the design load factor is exceeded the designer provides for a factor of safety and in the case of most aeroplanes this factor is 1.5 times the design limit load. Thus if the design limit load factor is 6 then the aircraft should be able to withstand an 'ultimate' load factor of 9g before structural collapse occurs. Nevertheless this is not an invitation to exceed the design load limits because permanent deformation and damage can occur to the airframe if the design load factor is exceeded. A further reason, and one that should be carefully considered by all aerobatic pilots, is that the safety factor of 1.5 will become degraded with the length of life of the airframe and the stresses to which it has been exposed.

Load factors are positive $(+)$ when a positive g is being pulled, as for example, in a steep turn or 'pull up' manoeuvre, and negative $(-)$ in the case of pushing the control column forward. High negative loadings are normally rare due to a resultant pilot discomfort in the abnormal attitudes required to achieve them, and because of this, aircraft need not be designed to withstand negative load factors to the same extent as is necessary with positive load factors. However aerobatics are manoeuvres which, if not properly controlled, can bring an aircraft close to the limiting edges of the V_n envelope. The lower load factors during negative g manoeuvres should therefore be kept in mind whenever negative g aerobatics are being carried out.

Referring to Fig. 7 it will be seen that the aircraft concerned has a limiting positive load factor of $6g$ and a limiting negative load factor of $3g$. The limiting airspeed (V_{ne}) is 200 knots IAS and the basic stalling speed (V_{s1}) is 50 knots. The curved lines extending out from the zero load factor represent the stall lines. These show the maximum load factors which can be applied at the various indicated airspeeds and the shape of these lines is based upon the fact that the stalling speed of an aeroplane increases directly with the square root of the load factor. Therefore if the basic stalling speed is 50 knots then at $4g$ it will stall at 100 knots and at $6g$ the stalling speed will be approximately 122 knots. In effect this means that no matter how much control force is applied by a pilot he would not be able to exceed $6g$ if the IAS was less than 122 knots because the aircraft would stall before this limiting load factor could be reached.

This fact leads to a consideration of an important speed which is normally defined for all modern general aviation aircraft as the 'manoeuvring speed' (V_A). This speed is the maximum speed at which the pilot can make abrupt and extreme control movements involving their full deflection without causing structural overloads. Above this speed, maximum deflection of the controls should not be used, because the pilot will be able to apply g forces in excess of the structural limitations.

Thus an aeroplane in flight is limited to operating within an envelope of airspeeds and load forces, one which does not exceed the limiting load factors, V_{ne} or maximum lift capabilty of the structure. To conclude it must be stressed that there are two major points of importance revealed in the V_g envelope. Point A in Fig. 7 shows the intersection of the positive maximum load factor and the line of positive maximum lift capability, and the airspeed at this intersection is the minimum airspeed at which the limiting load factor can be produced. Any airspeed greater than that shown at point A will produce a positive lift capability sufficient to cause damage to the aeroplane, and below this speed excessive flight loads cannot be induced. The same situation exists at point B when considering the negative limiting load forces.

In addition to the considerations covered in the previous paragraph, the information given earlier in relation to the effect of vertical gusts must also be kept in mind. For example if a pilot brings an aircraft close to its limiting load factor whilst carrying out an aerobatic manoeuvre in turbulent air, the combined effects of the pilot's control action and the turbulence could produce an eventual load factor in excess of the limiting figure.

Although an understanding of the contents of the previous paragraphs will help a pilot to avoid exceeding the limiting load factors on an aeroplane, he will nevertheless need certain facts and figures relating to the aircraft in which he is carrying out aerobatic manoeuvres. Operating Manuals for small general aviation aircraft do not contain diagrams of the type shown at Fig. 7. However they usually contain information relating to never exceed speed (V_{ne}) and manoeuvring speed (V_A). In the event that the latter figure is not shown it can be assessed from the following simple formula:

$$V_A = V_s \sqrt{n} \text{ limit}$$
$$\text{where } V_A = \text{Manoeuvre Speed}$$
$$V_s = \text{Stalling Speed}$$
$$n = \text{Limiting Load Factor}$$

This formula, when applied to the figures shown in Fig. 7 would appear as:

$$V_A = 50 \sqrt{6} = 122 \text{ knots}$$

THE ACCELEROMETER

Many of the aircraft which are cleared for aerobatics are equipped with an instrument known as an 'accelerometer' (or g meter). As the name implies, the instrument measures acceleration forces parallel to the vertical axis of the aircraft. It is essentially a spring balance device which measures the g forces on the aircraft (and the pilot), but because it is mounted on the approximate centre line of the fuselage it cannot give measurements of rolling *g* forces. The most commonly used type of accelerometer incorporates a 3 pointer display. One pointer gives an instantaneous read out of the actual *g* forces being applied at any time, which can be in the positive or negative sense. A second pointer measures the amount of positive *g* being applied and remains at the maximum value until reset. The third pointer has the same function as the second but in this case measures the maximum value of negative *g* which has been applied during the manoeuvre.

Fig. 8

Therefore after completing the manoeuvre the pilot can see the maximum positive and negative load factors which have been applied during the particular aerobatic exercise. The instrument incorporates a reset button which can be pushed to return the second and third pointers to the neutral reading of 1*g*. The instantaneous pointer reads the actual value of *g* being applied at any time (positive or negative) and is therefore not connected with the reset mechanism.

In level unaccelerated flight the aircraft and pilot are subject to the normal 1*g* load factor. If +3*g*s are pulled during a manoeuvre the change in the load factor will therefore be 2*g*. If −3*g* were applied the change in load factor would be 4*g*, i.e. +1*g* to −3*g* = a change of 4*g*s.

It will be appreciated that an accelerometer is an extremely useful device which will enable a pilot to establish the amount and direction of load factor which has been applied during a manoeuvre, as well as indicating the forces being applied at the time the manoeuvre is being carried out. Therefore it has great value to a pilot during an aerobatic manoeuvre in that he has the necessary warning to avoid overstressing the aircraft.

Finally, and from a practical viewpoint, it must be remembered that the load factors produced during aerobatic manoeuvres are placed on the entire aircraft structure and not just on its main components such as wing, spars, etc. As an aerobatic trainee you must bear in mind that an aeroplane is as strong as its weakest component, and experience has shown that most structural failures are due to excess load factors on rib structures of the leading and trailing edges of the main wings and tailplane. Additionally it is important to appreciate that the cumulative effect of excess loadings applied over a number of flights can tend to loosen and weaken vital components in a manner which can cause catastrophic failure at times when the aircraft is being operated well within its structural limitations. The performance of the basic aerobatic manoeuvres contained in this manual should not require *g* forces in excess of approximately 3.5*g*. However, it is of paramount importance, both to yourself and others who may subsequently fly the aircraft, that if at any time you exceed the load factor limitations, you place the aircraft unserviceable. It must not then be flown until the airframe has been inspected by a qualified aircraft engineer and any necessary rectification has been carried out.

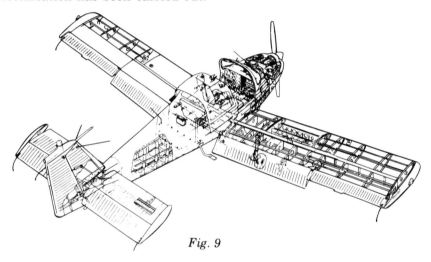

Fig. 9

ENGINE LIMITATIONS

Aircraft power plants are extremely rugged and reliable but they can nevertheless fail when handled improperly. Therefore good engine handling is a requirement for any aerobatic pilot. During aerobatic training and afterwards you will find your workload increases when carrying out the required manoeuvres and it is quite easy to forget the engine has limitations too, a common occurrence during aerobatics.

The tendency to make sudden and rapid power changes cannot be avoided during some of the aerobatic manoeuvres, but providing they are made smoothly and without exceeding the limiting RPM, the engine will accept this type of handling. The importance of avoiding sudden extremes of engine temperature is paramount, not only for you but also for those who may fly the aircraft afterwards. An aero engine is built to stand extremes of cold or heat but there is a limit at which an engine cannot accept a rapid change from cold to hot or vice

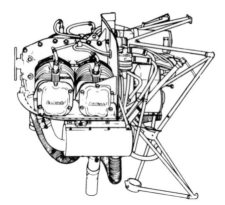

versa. Therefore it is essential not to apply full power rapidly following a situation where the engine has been allowed to cool to a low figure, such as during a descent with the throttle completely closed.

Failure to observe this important precaution can easily lead to the engine suffering damage, e.g., bent push rods, broken piston rings, cracked cylinders and warped and sticking exhaust valves, etc.

During your basic pilot training your instructor will have stressed the importance of making smooth rather than abrupt throttle movements and this philosophy is equally applicable during aerobatic training. Another item to stress is the habit of frequently confirming that engine oil pressure and temperature readings, and, when fitted, the cylinder head temperature readings, are within the required limits, as this can easily be forgotten during your early aerobatic training.

The 'redline' speed on the tachometer is another item which you will need to continuously monitor when increasing the power. The RPM with a fixed pitch propeller installation will vary considerably as the aircraft gains airspeed and your instructor will show you the airspeed where the full throttle RPM are just below the limiting figure. This will be of considerable assistance to you because during aerobatics you will be using the ASI at very frequent intervals.

In the event that the aircraft is equipped with a constant speed unit to govern the propeller RPM, you will need to take care not to overboost the engine. Your instructor will ensure you know the limiting manifold pressure/RPM range to stay within in these circumstances.

Another consideration relates to inverted flight. This manoeuvre is normally only permitted for a matter of a few seconds unless the engine has been specially designed or modified for operation in the inverted attitude. The aircraft in which you will be carrying out your basic aerobatic training will usually have certain restrictions limiting the use of inverted flight or sustained negative loadings. When inverted flight is permitted and the engine has not been adapted to run under these conditions there will be a loss of oil through the crankcase breather pipe and possible oil aeration as well. Therefore it will be necessary to check that the oil pressure reading is normal after any manoeuvre involving inverted flight, or whenever negative g has been imposed.

Additionally, most aerobatic training aircraft are equipped with a carburettor designed to function under positive g loadings. Under circumstances when the engine cuts due to the effect of negative g the throttle should be closed in order to ensure that the resumption of power does not occur abruptly, or at high RPM when the oil pressure may well be near zero.

PHYSICAL LIMITATIONS

Apart from knowing the limitations placed upon the airframe and engine, pilots who wish to become proficient in aerobatics must have a grasp of how these manoeuvres will affect the human body in relation to physical stresses, disorientation and airsickness. To commence aerobatic training without this knowledge can result in an unnecesary de-motivation or a reduced rate of progress in developing the skills required to perform these manoeuvres with accuracy and precision.

BODY STRESSES

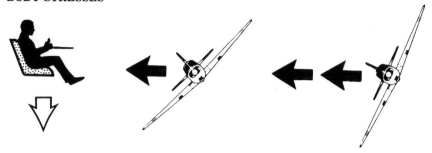

In normal level flight the aircraft and pilot are subjected to the normal gravitational pull (1g) which tends to accelerate a mass towards the centre of the earth. This normal force is something which is experienced by all humans whether they are standing still, sitting or flying in an aircraft. During flight, however, we can impose changes to this force on our bodies through self-induced acceleration. For example when an aircraft is placed in turning flight an acceleration will take place towards the centre of the turn. The greater the angle of bank, the steeper will be the curved path which the aircraft follows and the greater will be the acceleration. Apart from level turning flight an acceleration will also take place if we induce a curved path in the vertical plane, either upwards or downwards.

A simple example can be related to everyday life when standing in a lift which is rising or descending. When a lift starts to ascend we feel a 'heaviness' proportional to its rate of acceleration. When the lift reaches a constant velocity the acceleration returns to zero and our bodies are once more only subject to the normal force of 1g. If the lift were to accelerate downwards the weight of our bodies would feel less and we would be moving towards a negative g situation. A condition of zero g would apply if the downward acceleration was sufficient to produce the effect of weightlessness and any further downward acceleration would produce a negative g effect.

One of the physical effects on the body during these accelerations is that the blood, body organs, especially the heart, liver and intestines, tend to move along the line of acceleration whenever it is greater or less than 1g.

In the case of a positive g manoeuvre which produces a g force greater than +1 the blood and body organs move towards the lower limbs of the body and since the human brain relies upon a continuous circulation of blood (and the oxygen it contains) from the heart, there is a physiological limitation to the g force it can withstand and still continue to function properly.

During a 60° banked turn in level flight the load factor (g) is +2. In this turn the aircraft will change direction through 180° in 35 seconds. If now the bank was increased so that 180° was turned in 15 seconds the *g* force would increase to +5.

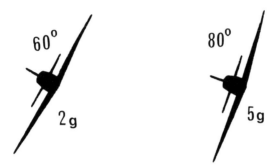

These same turning relationships will apply during aerobatics whether a pull force is applied in a 'vertical pull up' or in a horizontal direction. Typical basic aerobatic manoeuvres can produce *g* forces varying from just over 2*g* to 3.5*g*. It must nevertheless be borne in mind that more advanced manoeuvres can cause the *g* forces to reach significantly higher figures.

The effect of positive *g* manoeuvres is to cause a flow of blood away from the brain resulting in a loss of oxygen from this region. Due to the natural flexibility of the body organs and tissues coupled with the inertia of the blood, a slight delay in blood moving away from the brain occurs, and therefore the human body can withstand large *g* forces for a period of 2 or 3 seconds without ill effect. However if *g* forces greater than 3*g* are maintained for longer than a few seconds 'greying out' or 'spots before the eyes' will occur, particularly to pilots with little aerobatic experience. This effect and the actual *g* value at which it occurs will very much depend upon the pilot's physical condition and his aerobatic experience.

In any event, sustained *g* forces much above +3*g* will cause 'blacking out' and eventually unconsciousness. When this happens a pilot will of course be unable to continue the physical effort of pulling the *g* force, and this will then decrease which will lead to a return of consciousness. In the case of marked negative manoeuvres, the blood in the major arteries and veins will be forced upwards into the head and 'reddish' visual indications will occur. At higher values of negative *g* (−4.5*g* or more) unconsciousness can occur within a few seconds.

The approximate *g* tolerance limits which can be expected for pilots undergoing initial aerobatic training and the limits applicable to experienced aerobatic pilots are given in Tables 3 and 4.

Table 3   Inexperienced Aerobatic Pilots

Type of g	Direction of body movement	Aircraft manoeuvre	Time factor and effect
Positive +	Head to foot	Tight level turn or Pull out of dive	At $3g$ for 5 seconds greyout and spots before the eyes

Table 4   Experienced Aerobatic Pilots

Amount of g	Exposure time	Effects
+5	30 seconds	Blackout to unconsciousness
+4	1 minute	Greyout to unconsciousness
+3	3 minutes	Greyout to unconsciousness
−2	1 minute	Subjective discomfort to unconsciousness
−3	30 seconds	Respiratory distress to unconsciousness
−4	6 seconds	Head pains to unconsciousness

Centrifuge studies have shown that the human body can withstand forces of up to $12g$ for 2 to 3 seconds. With this fact in mind it can be seen that if a pilot causes a sudden increase of g it will be possible for him to exceed the load factor limitation of the aircraft before the effect of blood draining from the head and consequent loss of oxygen to the brain causes a blackout to occur.

This short review of the physiological effects which can occur during aerobatic flight is not intended to deter pilots from learning aerobatic manoeuvres, but rather to ensure they appreciate the sort of effects they can experience if they exceed their physical limitations. In summary the foregoing knowledge will be of value in two ways:

(1) It will give the prospective aerobatic pilot an appreciation of the natural physiological effects which may be met during aerobatic flight and create an awareness of the body's physical limitations.
(2) It demonstrates the need for caution and hopefully will prevent an over-zealous pilot exceeding his physical limitations particularly during the early stages of his aerobatic training.

Having made these two points it is also pertinent to state that human beings can progressively adapt their physical tolerance to body stresses imposed during aerobatics. Such increased tolerance can however only be achieved by maintaining a good physical condition and practising within safe limits. Equally any tolerance to g forces will always be reduced if the pilot is not in good physical shape, e.g., suffering from loss of sleep, effects of alcohol, etc.

Apart from the normal increase in tolerance to *g* manoeuvres which is obtained by experience, adaptation and maintaining a high state of physical fitness, a few pointers are given below which can further improve tolerance to positive *g* manoeuvres:

During the positive *g* manoeuvre:

● Tighten the stomach muscles.
● Hunch the body and lower the head.

Finally you must never forget that although the human body can withstand very high *g* forces for a brief interval of time, the airframe cannot, and if you pull more than the limiting *g* of your aircraft even for the shortest moment of time, the airframe will have been exposed to a damaging load factor.

DISORIENTATION AND AIRSICKNESS

Spatial disorientation is a condition which occurs when a pilot is confused about the attitude or motion of his aircraft due to false physical sensations. Mild and temporary disorientation is a fairly common experience during a pilot's initial training, but usually this is quickly overcome as a pilot adapts to the normal sensations of flight.

However, the markedly unusual attitudes, such as those involved during aerobatics give the pilot some very positive false bodily sensations during early training in these manoeuvres. The following paragraphs are written in order that you may understand why these sensations occur and how to combat them.

DISORIENTATION

We obtain the ability to interpret up and down and sideways movements through a combination of our physical senses. The human body employs many senses, but those which are primarily involved with orientation are the eyes, the balance mechanism in the ears, and the muscle, joint and skin receptors. When any confusion exists between these various senses the brain may be unable to interpret the messages being transmitted to it from these sources and disorientation is the result.

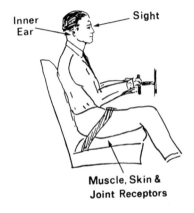

Inner Ear — Sight — Muscle, Skin & Joint Receptors

When this disorientation occurs during flight it is called 'spatial disorientation', the prefix 'spatial' being used to connect it with the environment of space, rather than man's natural habitat, the ground. Many flight situations may lead to the onset of spatial disorientation, but those which are most common are:

● A lack of flying practice.
● A lack of visual cues.
● Sudden head movements made at a time when the aircraft is rapidly changing its attitude in pitch, yaw or roll.
● Impairment of brain function due to lack of oxygen, effects of alcohol, fatigue, emotional disturbance or medication.
● Aerobatic manoeuvres (including spinning). Disorientation can occur either during these manoeuvres or immediately afterwards, and particularly during a sequence involving both looping and rolling motions.

Clearly the answer to a lack of flying practice is to avoid aerobatic manoeuvres until a period of normal flying has been undertaken and the body has become re-adjusted to in-flight sensations.

Because the eyes are the most powerful sense used in determining attitude, care should be taken to avoid carrying out aerobatics in conditions of poor visibility. It probably goes without saying that manoeuvres of this nature should also be conducted well away from clouds.

During their initial training most pilots will become aware of the false turning sensations which can be produced as a result of misleading sensations felt by the balance mechanism in the ears. This mechanism is the 'vestibular apparatus' located in the inner ear and consists of three semi-circular canals arranged at right angles to one another and which terminate in a common sac.

The canals and sac contain fluid and sensory hairs from which the sensations of balance are derived. The three canals are arranged so that one is in the vertical plane, one in the horizontal plane and one in the transverse plane. These planes can be related to the planes of movement of an aircraft in the manner shown in Fig. 10.

When the head is moved the fluid in the canals of each inner ear moves in the same direction and stimulates the sensory hairs giving them an appropriate impression of motion and direction, which is then transmitted to the brain. Without going into considerable detail, it can be stated that during flight, prolonged or sudden turning motions or sudden termination of a turning motion can result in erroneous impressions being received by the sensory hairs with resulting errors to the messages being transmitted to the brain. When this occurs a strong sense of disorientation will follow. This is the reason we feel a sense of dizziness and disorientation if we spin

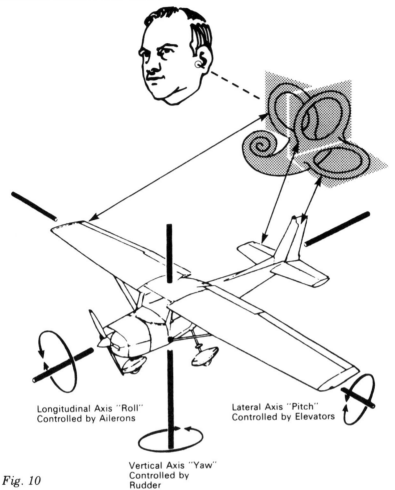

Longitudinal Axis "Roll"
Controlled by Ailerons

Lateral Axis "Pitch"
Controlled by Elevators

Vertical Axis "Yaw"
Controlled by
Rudder

Fig. 10

round several times and then suddenly stop.

An additional effect is that we have difficulty in maintaining balance until the movement of the fluid and its effect upon the sensory hairs within the balance mechanism stabilises again.

What is not always appreciated is that if an aircraft is turning in one direction and the pilot suddenly moves his head into the opposite direction, a stimulation of the balance mechanism will occur in two canals at the same time and spontaneously affect stimulation to the third. This leads to extremely confusing messages being received by the brain and severe disorientation can follow.

Similar effects of this sensation, known as 'coriolis stimulation' can be experienced when during a spin recovery a strong *g* force is applied whilst pulling out of the dive before the rolling motion has been stopped.

The subject of spatial disorientation can be developed at some length, but the intention of this manual is merely to ensure that the aerobatic trainee appreciates that disorientation can occur in many ways and be mild or powerful in effect. It is however a perfectly natural phenomenon and one in which the effects can be largely overcome by adaptation gained through experience. Although the effects are normally short lived all aerobatic pilots should know how best to avoid or reduce the onset of them.

Therefore to sum up so far:

● False sensations and sensory illusions may occur at any time during normal flight operations, but particularly when visual cues are inadequate. They are most marked when large changes of attitude are occurring in more than one plane, such as during aerobatic flight.

● The illusions can vary from being mild to very strong and in the latter case might easily lead to loss of control.

● Disorientation is aggravated by flight in conditions where a pilot is attempting to combine outside visual references with instrument flying references.

AIRSICKNESS

Apart from the temporary feeling of dizziness which is often an integral part of becoming disorientated, there is also the longer lasting effect of airsickness. Motion sickness is usually caused by continued stimulation of the balance mechanism of the inner ear, but it can also be aggravated by apprehension or anxiety. Therefore it can be appreciated that this type of sickness can be induced by many of the factors previously discussed in relation to disorientation.

Apart from the normal common sense precautions of avoiding large meals or fizzy drinks prior to flying, and having an adequately ventilated cockpit during flight, sickness can best be avoided by limiting the amount of aerobatic practice which is undertaken on any one flight. It will be possible to gradually extend the number of aerobatics practised as experience and confidence is gained.

With the previous information in mind it can be seen that the precautions which should be taken to minimise the physiological effects of aerobatic manoeuvres are:

● Make sure you are physically fit before attempting aerobatics and ensure you are free from the effects of anxiety, alcohol, medication and fatigue.

● Remain in flying practice and do not attempt aerobatics immediately following a lay-off from flying.

● Be aware of the fact that combined changes in the rolling, looping and yawing plane can be a particularly strong source of disorientation.

● Avoid rapid and large head movements when carrying out manoeuvres which involve a combination of motion about any two or more of the three axes.

LIMITATIONS APPLICABLE TO THE SPECIFIC AIRCRAFT TYPE

There are several makes and types of aircraft of both the high wing and low wing configuration which are suitable for aerobatic training. Some of these aircraft have a control wheel and others a control stick and although the use of high wing or low wing types, control wheels or sticks are more a matter for individual preference, the limitations laid down by the aircraft manufacturer must be regarded as mandatory or obligatory and should be abided by at all times.

In this respect the aircraft manual, whether it is called an Owner's Manual, Flight Manual or Pilot's Operating Handbook, must be your source of information relating to what the aircraft is permitted to do. Before attempting any type of aerobatic manoeuvre you must ensure, by reference to this manual (and any CAA Supplement it contains), that the aircraft has been cleared for the manoeuvre.

Additionally, and because many light aircraft are designed to be used in different operational categories (e.g. Normal, Utility, Semi-Aerobatic, and Aerobatic) the pilot will have to determine the 'all up weight' and centre of gravity position which permit him to use the aircraft in the semi-aerobatic or aerobatic category.

An example of how this information might appear in the aircraft manual is given below and in this case it relates to a Beagle Pup aircraft.

WEIGHT AND BALANCE:
Maximum weight for take-off, landing or aerobatics is 726 kg (1600 lb). The centre of gravity limits are shown on page 3–2 (*of the Aircraft Manual*). When aerobatics are carried out the aft centre of gravity limit is restricted as shown.

MANOEUVRES:
The aerobatic manoeuvres stated below are permitted with flaps retracted, provided that the centre of gravity range is restricted, that no baggage is carried and that both seats are provided with full safety harness. Otherwise the aeroplane is restricted to normal flying manoeuvres except that stalls may be carried out.

Aerobatic manoeuvres:
stalls, spins, inside loops, half roll and dive out, half loop and roll out, barrel rolls, slow rolls, flick rolls and stall turns.

Note: for engine considerations, inverted flight must be limited to a maximum duration of 20 seconds, with the throttle closed.

FLIGHT LOAD:
The maximum load factors which the aeroplane has been designed to withstand are:

Flaps up: Normal flight, $+3.8g$, $-1.44g$
                  Aerobatics, $+4.4g$, $-1.76g$

Flaps down: Normal flight, $+2.0g$

Manoeuvres shall be confined to those having load factors within these limits.

Note: this aeroplane has been designed and tested to the semi-aerobatic requirements of B.C.A.R. Section K.

BAGGAGE:
For normal flight the maximum permissible weight of baggage in the baggage compartment behind the seats is 38 kg (85 lb).

Maximum floor loading in the baggage compartment is 366 kg/m^2 (75 lb/ft^2).

No baggage may be carried during aerobatics.

WEIGHT AND BALANCE

LOADING
1. The moment envelope and the loading graph should be used to ensure that the centre of gravity limits are not exceeded.

BAGGAGE

MAX LOAD	**38 kg (85lb)**
FLOOR LOADING	**366 kg/M²**
	(75 lb/ft²)

**ALL LUGGAGE TO BE LASHED DOWN
NO BAGGAGE ALLOWED FOR
AEROBATICS**

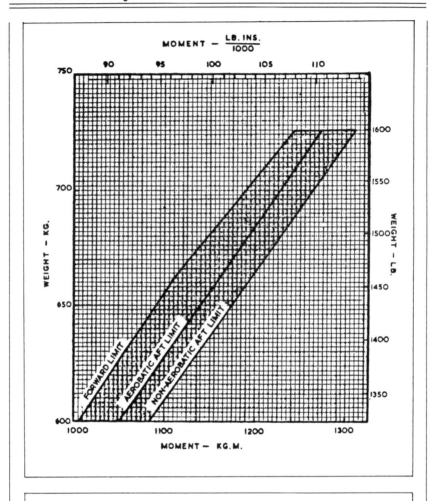

MOMENT — $\dfrac{\text{LB. INS.}}{1000}$

MOMENT — KG.M.

THIS AEROPLANE IS DESIGNED TO SEMI-AEROBATIC
LOAD FACTORS. WHEN PERFORMING
PERMITTED AEROBATICS CARE MUST BE TAKEN
NOT TO APPLY MORE g THAN IS NECESSARY.

The following aerobatic manoeuvres are permitted, the
recommended entry speeds (knots I.A.S.) are:

Loop	130
Barrel and slow rolls	120
Flick rolls	60 (max. 75)
Roll off the top	135
Half roll and dive out	80

The throttle must be closed during sustained inverted flight. Care must be taken not to exceed the maximum engine speed of 2750 rev/min in dives. During inverted flight oil is lost from the crankcase breather and oil aeration will also occur. After each period of negative g operation, a positive check must be made that the oil pressure has returned to normal (30–60 lb/in^2) before further negative g operation is commenced.

Flick rolls

The technique recommended for executing flick rolls is as follows:

With power on, apply full rudder and full up elevator simultaneously at the recommended air-speed.
Application of aileron in the direction in which rudder is applied will increase the rate of rotation, whereas application of aileron opposite to the direction in which rudder is applied will inhibit the manoeuvre.
The manoeuvre is stopped by centralising controls.
If the manoeuvre is mishandled at low airspeed a spin may result; close the throttle and take normal spin recovery action.

A further example of how information relating to the limitations for aerobatic flight is shown in these extracts from a Fuji FA 200-160 aircraft manual.

THE APPROVED AEROBATIC MANOEUVRES
1. Fuel boost pump 'on' (and in case of fuel selector valve system, turn it to left) during aerobatic flight.
2. Do not keep inverted attitude. Inverted flight is prohibited.
Aerobatic category maximum weight 1940 lb
Aerobatic manoeuvres are limited to the following.

Manoeuvres	*Entry Speed*
Chandelle	135 mph (117 knots)
Lazy 8	135 mph (117 knots)
Steep turn	135 mph (117 knots)
Stall (except whip stall)	slow deceleration
Loop	150 mph (130 knots)
Cuban 8	150 mph (130 knots)
Immelmann turn	150 mph (130 knots)
Clover leaf	150 mph (130 knots)
Aileron roll	130 mph (113 knots)

Barrel roll   130 mph (113 knots)
Snap roll   100 mph (87 knots)
Wing over   110 mph (96 knots)
Hammer head stall   110 mph (96 knots)
Spins (flap up, engine idle)   slow deceleration
Utility category max. weight 2137 lb
Aerobatic manoeuvres are limited to the following.
Stall (except whip stall), steep turn, lazy 8, chandelle, spins (flap up, engine idle)

Normal category max. weight   2335 lb for 7656 propeller
                                  2270 lb for 7662 propeller

No aerobatic manoeuvres including spins approved

Airspeed indicator markings are marked for Normal or Utility category. For aerobatic category, see the approved aeroplane flight manual

---

(2) Demonstrated cross-wind and design manoeuvring speed on the instrument panel and full view of pilot.

(3) Flap extended speed on the flap handle.

The design manoeuvring speed
Normal and Utility category
   134 mph (116 kt)
Aerobatic category 148 mph
   (128 kt)
The demonstrated cross wind
   15 knots

Flap extended speed
15° 139 mph (121 knot)
25°, 35° 119 mph (103 knot)

---

(4) Baggage shelf
On the side wall of baggage shelf
(S/N FA-200-13 ~ 19
FA-200-244 and after)

(5) Baggage room
On the door of
baggage room
(S/N FA-200-244
and after)

Maximum baggage weight
  20 kg or 44 lb
Baggage shelf
No baggage in aerobatic
  flight

Maximum baggage weight
  80 kg or 176 lb
Baggage room
No baggage in aerobatic
  flight

(S/N FA-200-23 ~ 243)

Maximum baggage weight
  40 kg or 88 lb
Baggage shelf
No baggage in aerobatic
  flight

Apply to S/N FA-200-13 ~ FA-200-243, except FA-200-102

2-7-3 Flight load factor

Category	Limited flight load factor	
	Flap up	Flap down
N	+3.8 ~ −1.52	
U	+4.4 ~ −1.76	+2.0
A	+6.0 ~ −3.0	

2-7-4 Number of crew
     Maximum:
          N Category 4
          U Category 3
          A Category 2
     Minimum: 1
     In case of 3 crew, 2 front and 1 rear.

CAUTION

> Inverted flight manoeuvres are prohibited.
> This condition should be avoided as much as possible due to wet sump engine oil system and carburetter type fuel system.
> Even if conducting the approved manoeuvres, be careful not to cause negative g on the aeroplane.

II Cautions and limitations to be observed during aerobatic flight

1. The aeroplane weight must be within the limits specified in para. 2-7 of this manual.
2. Gyro horizon and directional gyro with cage mechanism incorporated should be caged, and all loose equipment should be stowed securely.
3. Before entry of aerobatic manoeuvres, set fuel booster pump 'ON' and (if installed*) set fuel selector valve 'LEFT'.
4. The use of flaps in the execution of approved aerobatic manoeuvres is prohibited.
5. The safety entry speed specified in para. 2-7 of this manual should be strictly observed.
6. The flight load factor specified in para. 2-7 of this manual should be strictly observed.
7. Care should be exercised to prevent the engine speeds from exceeding 2700 RPM (max).
8. Continuous diving should be avoided not to exceed 172 mph IAS (V_{ne}).
9. Proper control technique should be performed for aircraft attitude change due to effect of propeller stream during aerobatic manoeuvre.
10. If a spin is entered inadvertently from an aerobatic manoeuvre, it is important to close the throttle to idle promptly and to take the spin recovery procedure.

*S/N FA-200-243 and before.

A further point which should be noted is that the method of presenting weight and centre of gravity graphs or tables will vary between the aircraft manuals for various types of aircraft. These differences are clearly seen by referring to the c.g. graphs previously illustrated for the Beagle Pup and Fuji aircraft and comparing these with the method of c.g. calculations for the Slingsby T67 shown as follows:

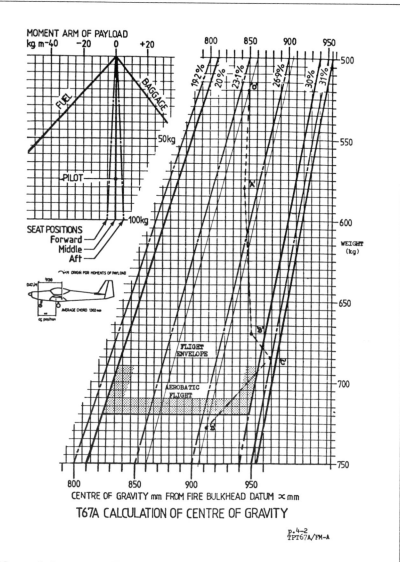

T67A CALCULATION OF CENTRE OF GRAVITY

p.4-2
TPT67A/FM-A

Normal Operating Procedure

Verification of Loading

The verification of the loading allows one to check that the aircraft is loaded within the centre of gravity and maximum total weight limitations.

The verification is carried out by calculating the centre of gravity as shown hereunder. The procedure is illustrated by the following example:

Let the loading be:
  1 pilot weight 60 kg with seat in forward position;
  1 pilot weight 90 kg with seat in rearward position;
  Luggage: 15 kg;
  Fuel: 60 litres ($\times$ 0.72 = 43 kg).

From the origin O, defined by the weight and centre of gravity of the empty aircraft, draw a line parallel to 'forward pilot' with a length OA corresponding to 60 kg on the diagram.

From point A draw a further line parallel to 'rearward pilot' of length AB corresponding to 90 kg. Proceed similarly for the luggage (vector BC) and fuel (vector CD). This gives the final weight and centre of gravity position at point D showing that the weight is 728 kg and centre of gravity is 906 mm.

N.B. In practice for the pilots it is normally sufficient to use the average of the two seat position scales.

Important: Since the fuel will be used up during the flight, it is necessary to verify that the centre of gravity with zero fuel lies within the normal centre of gravity range limitation.

Maximum Take-off and Landing Weights

The maximum all up weight is 750 kg.
Aerobatic manoeuvre prohibited for weights in excess of 720 kg.

Centre of Gravity

The horizontal datum is the top of fuselage upper spar forming the cockpit sill. The fore and aft datum for the centre of gravity is the forward face of the bulkhead firewall.

Limits of Centre of Gravity

	Aircraft MPTW	Distance aft of datum
Forward limit	750 kg (1650 lb)	x = 810 mm (2 ft 8 in)
Aft limit	720 kg (1584 lb)	x = 940 mm (3 ft 1 in)
Aft limit	750 kg (1650 lb)	x = 953 mm (3 ft $1\frac{1}{2}$ in)

Limits	Manoeuvres for MTWA 720 kg (1584 lb)	
	Entry Speeds (IAS)	
Never exceed speed V_{ne} 138 knots (IAS)	Stabilised inverted flight and turns	70 knots
Manoeuvring speed V_A 123 knots (IAS)	Entry to and exit from inverted flight	80 knots
Flap operating speed 92 knots (IAS)	Slow roll	113 knots
Maximum total 720 kg 750 kg Weight authorised (1584 lb) (1650 lb)	Stall turn entry	113 knots
	Stall turn rotate	43 knots
Max g load Flaps up +6 −3 +4.4 −1.8 Flaps down +2 +2	Loop	108 knots
	Roll off the top	123 knots
Loss of height to recover from stall : 150 feet (46 m)	Flick roll max	70 knots
	Spin − See Flight Manual	
Flight in known icing conditions is prohibited	Powered inverted flight prohibited	
The aircraft is certified for daytime VFR flight only.		

Another important point to bear in mind in relation to aircraft manual information, is that foreign manufactured aircraft which are certificated in the UK are required to meet certain British Civil Airworthiness requirements. Upon certification, the Airworthiness Section of the CAA will usually require a Supplement to be inserted in the aircraft manual. This Supplement will often contain changes to the manufacturer's operating instructions and limitations and should be studied by the pilot to see whether any of the information it contains affects the aerobatic or other limitations or instructions.

The various limitations appropriate to the aircraft being used in your training will be covered by the instructor during your course, but once qualified, these facts and figures will have to be discovered on your own. It is important therefore that you are aware of the variations in the method of presenting this information in the

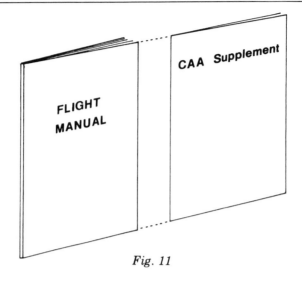

Fig. 11

different aircraft manuals, and you should not hesitate to obtain advice in this area before carrying out aerobatic manoeuvres in any aircraft with which you are unfamiliar.

AIRSPEEDS

A competent aerobatic pilot will avoid using an airspeed in excess of that normally required to perform a specific aerobatic manoeuvre, nevertheless your instructor may initially suggest the use of entry speeds which are slightly higher than those which are recommended. The purpose of this is to give you greater control over the aircraft throughout the lower speed section of the manoeuvre during your initial practice, e.g. at the top of a loop where the airspeed will have dropped to a very low figure. However, the slightly higher entry speeds suggested by your instructor should always be within structural limitations.

Note: In most aircraft the minimum speed for entering a loop, aileron roll, barrel roll or stall turn will be approximately 3 times the indicated stall speed (V_{s1}). Below this figure it is unlikely that the manoeuvre could be performed satisfactorily.

Many early aircraft had very high drag factors and it was usually difficult to inadvertently exceed the V_{ne} during the aerobatic diving manoeuvres. However the modern light aircraft has very clean lines and a low drag factor, therefore extreme care will often be necessary to avoid exceeding the V_{ne} whilst executing the dive section following entry to a manoeuvre. In aircraft fitted with fixed pitch propellers an increase of airspeed will cause an increase in RPM and this too will have to be borne in mind during the high speed section of a manoeuvre in order that the limiting RPM is not exceeded.

ENGINE

The general considerations relating to engine handling during aerobatic manoeuvres have already been covered in an earlier section of this manual, therefore all that need be said under this heading is that a pilot must again make reference to the aircraft manual and determine the specific limitations and engine handling instructions.

THE ARESTI SYSTEM

The Aresti aerocryptographic system of notation and classification of aerobatic manoeuvres was developed by Colonel J. Aresti, a Spanish Air Force instructor, during the 1950s. Prior to this pilots used a multiplicity of personal lists or diagrams to portray their aerobatic manoeuvre sequences. The international acceptance of the Aresti system has led to far easier interpretation of aerobatic sequences without any language problem.

The basis of the system is that of lines and angles connecting manoeuvres both on the 'X' and 'Y' axes of the aerobatic judging box. Horizontal, vertical and 45° lines, erect, inverted and knife edge flight are depicted as follows:

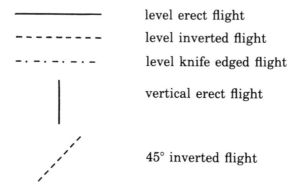

————————	level erect flight
– – – – – – – –	level inverted flight
– · – · – · – · –	level knife edged flight
	vertical erect flight
	45° inverted flight

A figure commences with a dot and terminates with a short stroke, i.e.　　∘– – – – – – – –ı

Lines, angles and manoeuvres on the 'Y' axis are drawn at 30° in a form of isometric projection, i.e.

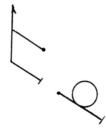

The complete Aresti dictionary portrays in excess of 70 000 different figures made up of pitching, rolling, yawed or snap/spin manoeuvres in various combinations. To each it gives a classification and a difficulty factor. All serious competitive aerobatic pilots need access to the current issue of the directory which is available through the British Aerobatic Association.

Aresti notation for the manoeuvres contained within the AOPA aerobatic certificate training course syllabus is shown in Table 5.

Table 5   Aresti Notation

Difficulty factor (K Value)	Symbol	Description	Aresti classification
K 12		Loop	7.1.1.
K 10		Aileron or slow roll	8.1.1.1.1.
K 10		Barrel roll	8.1.3.1.1.
K 3		Steep turn through 270°	2.2.
K 20		Stall turn	5.1.1.
K 16		Half Cuban 8	9.1.1.2.
K 18		Half reverse Cuban 8	2.1.2.1.

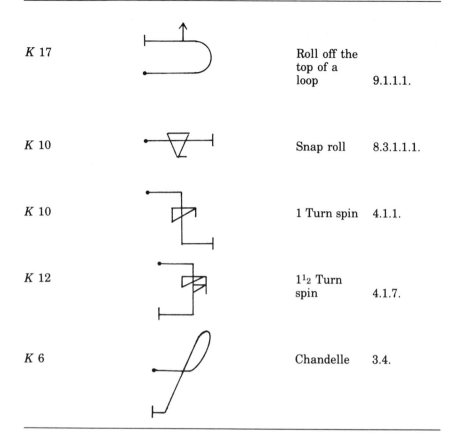

K 17		Roll off the top of a loop	9.1.1.1.
K 10		Snap roll	8.3.1.1.1.
K 10		1 Turn spin	4.1.1.
K 12		1¹₂ Turn spin	4.1.7.
K 6		Chandelle	3.4.

A typical sequence drawn for the above manoeuvres might be as follows:

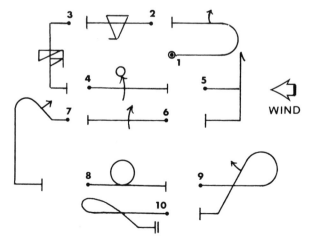

K value

17	1.	Roll off the top
10	2.	Snap roll
12	3.	$1^1{}_2$ Turn spin
10	4.	Barrel roll
20	5.	Stall turn
10	6.	Aileron or slow roll
18	7.	½ Reverse Cuban (flown as half climbing roll $+\frac{5}{8}$ loop)
12	8.	Loop
16	9.	½ Cuban
6	10.	Chandelle

Total 131

At each figure the entry speed and height margin must be considered with strict observance to base height 'break off'. A well designed sequence will ensure that the exit speed from one figure will be the entry speed for the next. It will also make allowance for the effect of wind on the shape of the figures and flight path lines.

Initially one should design two figure sequences and then link two sets of these to give a progression of 2, 4, 6 and 8 in various orders. Eventually on entering competition aerobatics the flown sequence will be assessed by a panel of ground-based judges, however the initial appraisal is likely to be from your instructor in the air.

The aerobatic area is a box in the sky measuring 1000 metres × 1000 metres × 900 metres deep. Its depth will often be constrained by airspace and aircraft performance limitations since, initially the base height will be at 3000 feet above ground level.

To utilise the 'Y' axis a 90° change of direction can be obtained by a steep turn through 90° or 270°. Alternatively a $1\frac{1}{4}$ turn spin or even a $\frac{1}{4}$ clover leaf could be used, the latter consisting of a manoeuvre where the aircraft is rolled vertically through 90° after the first quarter of a loop and then continuing with the loop.

Lines and angles in the judging criteria must be cleanly drawn in the sky and a common early fault by competitive pilots is to blur the figures together by not hesitating briefly in the level, 45° or vertical flight path.

Commencement of a sequence is by signalling a double 'wing rock' of at least 30° with a single wing rock upon completion. In competitive aerobatics marks are given out of 10 for each figure which itself is allocated a difficulty coefficient. These are multiplied to give a value for the figure and the totals added for a final sequence mark. Penalties for breaks and height infringements are deducted at

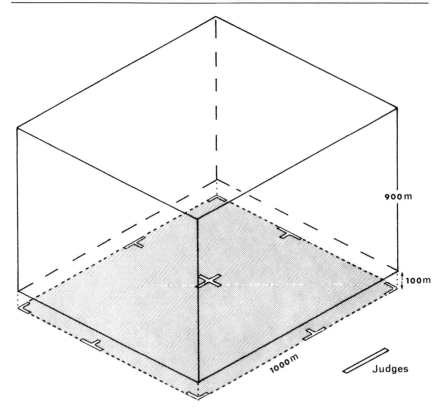

this point. The contestant with the maximum number of points is declared the winner. Contests are usually set with a number of sequences. These consist of:

Group 1.   Known compulsory sequence.
Group 2.   Free sequence with maximum K factor specified.
Group 3.   Unknown compulsory sequence.
Group 4.   Four minute free sequence.

At standard level it is normal to fly Group 1 with only occasionally Group 3 in addition. The 'intermediate' level usually includes both Group 1 and 3, and 'advanced' and 'unlimited' levels will probably include Groups 1, 2 and 3 together with Group 4 on certain occasions.

The British Aerobatic Association contests are set with the following minimum performance aircraft in mind:

Standard level   Tiger Moth or Cessna Aerobat
Intermediate level   Stampe and Jungmeister
Advanced level   CAP 10 and Zlin
Unlimited level   Pitts and CAP 21

Group 1 sequences are set with the following K values as a target:

Standard	100 to 150 K
Intermediate	200 to 250 K
Advanced	300 to 400 K
Unlimited	500 to 600 K

Long Briefings and Air Exercises

Long Briefings and Air Exercises

PRE-AEROBATIC REVISION

Airmanship considerations
Advanced turning
Slow flight
Stalling
Spinning – recovery at the incipient stage
The spiral dive

The considerations and principles involved in the performance of the above exercises have all been covered in detail in the AOPA Training Manual for the Private Pilot's Licence. Consequently it is not intended to give more than a brief summary of the important factors concerning these manoeuvres in this manual. You may therefore find it useful to revise the information in the basic Private Pilot Training Manual before commencing the first stage of your aerobatic training.

AEROBATIC EXERCISES

Developed spins
Lazy 8s
Chandelles
Recoveries from markedly unusual attitudes
Re-starting the engine 'In flight' (as applicable)
Loop
Aileron roll
Barrel roll
Slow roll
Stall turn
Half Cuban 8
Reverse half Cuban 8
Roll off the top of a loop
Snap roll
Combination manoeuvres

Flight Training

AIRMANSHIP

An extremely high standard of airmanship is required from any aspiring aerobatic pilot and because the meaning of the word 'airmanship' covers many aspects it is outlined under several sub-headings as follows:

Lookout

During aerobatics an aircraft will be involved in rapid changes of airspeed, altitude, direction and attitude, therefore the pilot of another aircraft will often have difficulty in assessing the parameters upon which he can base his own avoiding actions. To determine a course of avoiding action upon sighting an aircraft which is in sustained level, climbing, descending or turning flight is normally a straightforward matter, but it is obviously far less simple when sighting an aircraft which is in the process of carrying out aerobatic manoeuvres.

Therefore prior to aerobatic manoeuvres the pilot must be especially careful to ensure that the area being used for these manoeuvres is completely free of other aircraft, both vertically and horizontally. All pilots will have been trained to carry out a careful lookout before practising stalling or spinning, where the emphasis was on the area immediately surrounding the aircraft and particularly below. When engaging in aerobatics however, the search area surrounding the aircraft must be significantly increased in the horizontal, as well as vertically above and below the aircraft.

Once the aerobatic manoeuvre is commenced the difficulty of maintaining an adequate lookout is increased and if another aircraft enters the area of airspace being used for the manoeuvre a very real danger of collision will exist.

An extremely thorough sky search must therefore be made and aerobatics should not be commenced until you have ensured the area is completely free of other aircraft.

Altitude

The fact that there is no legal requirement to maintain a specific minimum height above the surface (with the exception of height over towns and the low flying rule) should not be accepted as a clearance to carry out aerobatics below a sensible minimum level. Safety considerations for the pilot and those people on the ground demand that a safe altitude (at least 3000 ft agl) be adhered to, and in this respect it will be of value to consider how quickly an aircraft can reach the surface when travelling at, say, 120 knots in a dive. Although there are other factors which affect this altitude consideration, e.g. inadvertent loss of control, unintentional spins, etc., Fig. 12 should bring home to any pilot the serious consequences of having insufficient height when carrying out aerobatics.

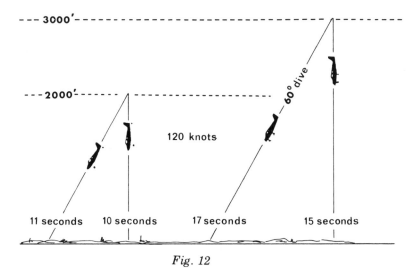

Fig. 12

Whereas most people become reasonably proficient at estimating horizontal distance by the time they commence their pilot training, the appreciation of height as a distance is not an estimation which is commonly employed. It would assist this appreciation if one were to consider that 3000 ft is usually less than the take-off distance available at many aerodromes used for training so just before your next take-off look along the line of take-off distance available and imagine this length stood on its end. From this you will quickly see that a distance of 3000 ft above the surface is not very far when you have to sort yourself out from an aerobatic manoeuvre which has gone wrong.

The message is clear – never practise aerobatic manoeuvres at less than 3000 ft above the surface and use a higher altitude if at all possible. The fact that competition pilots operate at lower levels should not influence your own minimums because these pilots have had far greater training and acquired considerable experience.

Loose Articles
Prior to strapping himself in before flight, the pilot must ensure that there are no loose articles present in the cockpit or cabin and that items such as first aid kits, fire extinguishers, etc., are firmly secured in a safe position. If the aircraft is equipped with a control lock device it must not be stowed in a slit pocket on the side of the cockpit or the back of a seat, as it could easily slip out of this kind of stowage.

Additionally, pilots often carry items in their pockets and such objects as coins can easily fall out during inverted manoeuvres and finish up by fouling the control cables, pulleys, etc. This possibility applies whether the aircraft has a control wheel system or a control stick, so considerable care must be taken in this respect. An extremely careful search should be made throughout the cockpit/cabin to ensure that pencils, clipboards, tools, etc., have not been left by the last person who flew the aircraft or the maintenance engineers who worked on the aircraft. It is not uncommon for articles like these to be found loose in aircraft.

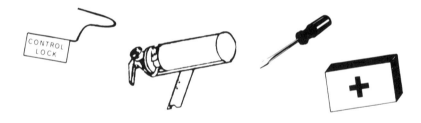

Loose articles can kill

Security and adjustment of harnesses
There are several types of harness fitted to aerobatic aircraft and it is vital that these are fastened correctly and properly adjusted prior to any type of aerobatic flight. Because this manual is written for the pilot who is carrying out initial aerobatic training rather than for the more advanced competition pilot, the following comments are centred around the types of harness more commonly found in those aircraft which are used for basic aerobatic training.

The basic harness consists of four straps, two of which secure the lower torso to the seat and two which secure the upper torso. Apart from the importance of ensuring that you know how to lock these straps into position it is also necessary to know the order and method of tightening the straps around the body, therefore you should note the following procedure:

(1) Before tightening any straps the seat should (if it is adjustable in the vertical) be in a slightly lower position than that which the pilot would normally use in flight.

(2) The lower torso straps should be tightened first and for aerobatics this does mean very tight – to the extent that it is rather uncomfortable. However when tightening these straps the pilot must ensure that he has an adequate range of leg movement in order to operate the rudder pedals to their full extent. This will normally entail adjusting the rudder pedals, or the fore and aft position of the seat.

(3) Once the lower torso straps have been adjusted the upper torso straps can be tightened, but not so much as to make it difficult to reach the various cockpit controls and systems.

(4) In the case of seats which can be adjusted in the vertical sense, the seat should now be raised to the position normally used by the pilot, this action will increase the tension on the straps and ensure the body is fully restrained.

Bear in mind that however tightly the straps are adjusted initially, they will tend to loosen off slightly during flight, and will need further tightening just prior to commencing aerobatic manoeuvres, and also at intervals during the flight.

Aerobatic Area

The area used for aerobatic training must be well clear of towns, active aerodromes, controlled airspace, danger areas, etc. Be particularly careful to avoid known let down areas to aerodromes, because when pilots are carrying out the aerodrome approach phase of flight, cockpit workloads can be high and their lookout less efficient.

Stay well clear of clouds and avoid approaching within 1000 ft of cloud tops and bases. Many General Aviation aircraft which are climbing or descending through cloud will travel about 1000 ft in 5 seconds, therefore it is a wise rule to keep well away from clouds during aerobatic manoeuvres.

ADVANCED TURNING

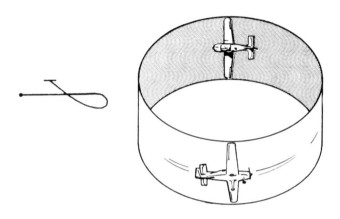

OBJECTIVES

The abillty to carry out steep turns will have been developed during your training for the basic Private Pilot Licence. Advanced turning has however been included in the aerobatic syllabus as it may have been some time since you practised this manoeuvre. Competence in precision steep turns is a valuable step towards improving your handling skills, particularly in situations where more than normal *g* forces are involved. The main objectives in this exercise will therefore be to:

(1) Give you some concentrated revision at improving co-ordination skills.
(2) Develop greater confidence in controlling the aircraft during manoeuvres involving steeply banked attitudes, and increased *g* forces.
(3) Develop greater precision in relation to rolling out from the turn onto specific headings.
(4) Give you practice at handling an aircraft in sustained steep turns close to the stalling speed and at rates of turn which are closer to the aircraft's structural limitations.

STEEP LEVEL, DESCENDING AND CLIMBING TURNS

Steep angles of bank can be achieved during level, descending or climbing flight, but an increased rate of turn will only be possible in the descending turn providing structural limitations permit. This is because the accelerating effect of gravity while descending makes more power available to maintain the aircraft in the turn. Conversely, because more power is required to climb the aircraft it can be appreciated that the maximum rate of turn attainable in a climb will be less than during level flight.

Load Factor

Bear in mind that in a level turn the load factor increases with angle of bank, and notwithstanding that the power available may become the first limiting factor, the maximum angle of bank which could be used when altitude is maintained will be dependent upon the limiting positive load factor for the aircraft concerned, e.g. if the limiting load factor is +4.4g then a maximum angle of bank will be approximately 75°.

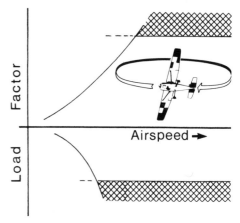

Increased stalling speed

During the turn at constant speed and altitude, the angle of attack will have to be increased to produce the extra lift required to support the aircraft. This causes an increase in the stalling speed which is directly related to the bank angle. Figure 13 illustrates the percentage variation of stall speed with angle of bank.

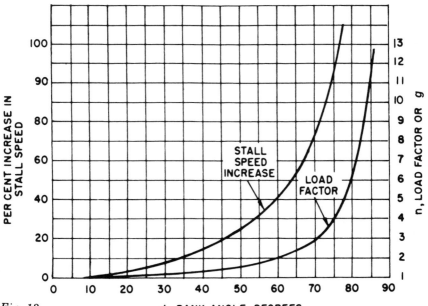

Fig. 13

Therefore as the bank angle is increased two factors of importance occur, both the stalling speed and the drag increase. The increase in drag will cause the airspeed to decrease unless sufficient power is available to combat the added drag and keep the airspeed constant. It can therefore be seen that if insufficient power is available to overcome the additional drag the flying speed will move toward the already increasing stalling speed as the angle of bank increases. A condition of stall will then occur at a substantially higher speed than that experienced when the aircraft is flown in a condition where the load factor is 1.

FLIGHT EXERCISE

ENTRY AND MAINTAINING THE STEEP LEVEL TURN

Having first ascertained the aircraft position in relation to known landmarks, and ensured that the surrounding airspace is clear of other air traffic, note the airspeed and initiate the entry in exactly the same way as for a medium level turn. As the bank angle reaches 30° increase the power, and continue the roll to 45° bank angle whilst increasing the back pressure on the control column. Later, as proficiency is increased, steep turns at angles of bank of 60° should be practised.

The added power should be just enough to maintain the airspeed and the increased back pressure sufficient to maintain the altitude. Rudder should be used throughout to maintain the aircraft in a balanced condition. During the steep turn the controls are all used in the same way as for normal turns.

Whilst one aim during the practice of steep turns will be to maintain altitude, it is important not to achieve this at the expense of airspeed, and whilst small variations in speed are acceptable, it should be remembered that a significant lowering of airspeed can lead to a stall condition. Therefore if altitude is being lost whilst speed is being maintained, further power will be required as well as an adjustment to back pressure. Simply adjusting the nose to a higher pitch attitude will result in a decrease of airspeed, leading to a decrease in lift and after a short while the aircraft will start losing altitude again.

Whereas small changes in airspeed are controlled in the normal way by use of the elevators, if altitude is being lost and the airspeed is increasing significantly in relation to the entry airspeed, then application of back pressure alone will also serve to tighten the turn due to the steepness of the bank attitude. This will lead to a tendency for the nose to drop still further and the airspeed to continue to increase. This is the beginning of a spiral dive during which structural limitations can easily be exceeded. The only correct method of recovery will be to decrease the bank at the same time as the added back pressure is applied and when the attitude in pitch has been readjusted any required increase in bank angle can be re-applied using the controls in the same way as for the entry.

RECOVERY FROM THE STEEP LEVEL TURN

This is effected by using the controls in the normal way, and reducing the power at the same time and as this is an exercise in advanced co-ordination the power reduction should be timed so that the cruising RPM setting is achieved as the wings become level. Due to the added back pressure required during the turn, care should be taken to release all of this back pressure progressively during the roll out or the aircraft will commence to climb as the bank is reduced.

The object throughout is to achieve a smooth manoeuvre, and hurried entries or recoveries should be avoided. Later, as a higher level of competence is achieved quicker entries and recoveries can be practised, but again it must be stressed that smooth and balanced flight will always be the requirement in practice situations.

THE STEEP DESCENDING TURN

These turns will be practised from powered descents or glides. The control functions are exactly the same as for steep level turns, but due to the lower nose attitude in relation to the horizon line (particularly in the gliding case) it will be a little more difficult to maintain a constant airspeed. With descending steep turns the entry airspeed should be higher than for a normal glide descent, and this speed increase should be in relation to the pre-selected bank angle, i.e. the higher the intended bank angle the higher the airspeed. This is to ensure an adequate margin above the increased stalling speed during the turn.

Referring to Fig. 13 the increase of stall speed at 45° is 18% and at 60° is 40%. Ignoring power effects on the stalling speed and assuming a V_{s1} of 50 knots this will mean that at 45° of bank the stalling speed will have increased to 59 knots and at 60° of bank to 70 knots. Therefore a good rule of thumb would be to increase the normal descent or glide speed by 10 knots for a 45° banked turn and 20 knots for a 60° banked turn.

During steep descending turns the tendency for the nose to lower will be more marked and a quicker reaction to this must be made by bank reduction and an increase in back pressure.

THE STEEP CLIMBING TURN

The use of full power will be needed if not already being used during the climb. The amount by which the angle of bank used impairs the rate of climb will depend upon the excess horsepower available for the particular aircraft, but the object will be to practise this type of steep turn up to bank angles of 40° to 45°.

Higher bank angles usually lead to a large reduction in climb rate and result in a situation where the aircraft is doing a steep turn with a higher than normal nose attitude and a very small rate of climb. The normal climbing speed will be appreciably lower than the entry speed for a level steep turn, so the considerations in relation to an increased stall speed will apply and care must be used to avoid a stall occurring.

MAXIMUM RATE TURNS

The turning performance of an aircraft can be related to the maximum rate and the minimum radius of turn. The rate of turn at any given airspeed will depend upon the accelerating force available for the turn and this will be provided by the horizontal component of the lift. Lift is a product of airspeed and angle of attack and will be at maximum when the aircraft is flying at the highest airspeed and just below the stalling speed for the load factor being applied.

The turning capability of any aircraft will therefore be limited by three basic factors:

The maximum lift capability.
The maximum power available.
The airframe load factor limitations.

For the case of the steady co-ordinated turn at a constant altitude the vertical component of lift must equal the weight. The additional total lift required when the aircraft is operating at large angles of bank is considerably greater than when carrying out medium banked turns. For example, at 60° of bank the total lift requirement to maintain the turn and remain at a constant height is twice that required for level flight, and at 75° of bank the lift requirement will be four times as great.

The pilot can obtain the additional lift by increasing the angle of attack through the application of back pressure on the control column during the turn. However, at the high angles of attack required to produce the large increases in total lift the induced drag is considerable, resulting in very positive reductions in airspeed which in turn lead to a reduction of the lift which could otherwise have been maintained. Typical values of increases in the induced drag during a level steep turn are as follows:

At 45° of bank the induced drag is increased by 100%.
At 60° of bank the induced drag is increased by 300%.

Thus there will be a limiting angle of bank at which the power available is no longer able to overcome the drag and the airspeed and

consequently the lift will start to decrease unless altitude is lost in order to maintain the airspeed. Any attempt to increase the rate of turn by descending must however be considered in relation to the limiting structural load factor. For example, it can be seen by reference to Fig. 13 that an aircraft cleared to $+6g$ will meet its limiting load factor during a level steep turn at 80° of bank. Therefore an attempt to increase the rate of turn beyond this point will lead to structural damage.

Normally light aircraft will not have sufficient power available to sustain a steep turn beyond 80° during level flight, but in the case of those aircraft used for aerobatics which have a limiting load factor of $+4.4g$ the structural limitation will prohibit level turns being carried out above 75° of bank and any attempt to increase the rate of turn by descending could easily lead to a dangerous situation.

In summary you should appreciate that provided the limiting load factor is not exceeded, the maximum rate and the minimum radius of turn will be achieved by using:

Maximum power.
Maximum angle of bank.
Maximum airspeed just below the stall speed for the applied load factor.

PRECISION STEEP TURNS

The objective in a precision steep turn is to recover onto a specific heading as accurately as possible. This must be accomplished so that the wings regain lateral level at the same time as the required heading is reached and extremely good control co-ordination is needed to ensure that both balance and altitude is maintained during the recovery to straight and level flight. The exercise will take a little time to perfect but it is an excellent co-ordination manoeuvre in preparation for basic aerobatics and precision spin recoveries.

Clearly the accent will be on the timing of control movements during the roll out phase and this will vary depending upon the aircraft type and the angle of bank being used in the turn.

SLOW FLIGHT

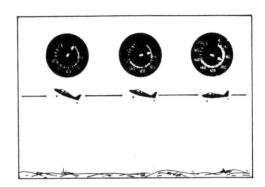

OBJECTIVES

During many aerobatic manoeuvres the aircraft will have to be controlled at very low airspeeds. The ability to maintain balanced flight while safely controlling the aircraft at low speeds will only be achieved through practice. This practice will be more beneficial if the aircraft is maintained in a slow flight condition for longer periods than those experienced solely during an aerobatic manoeuvre. Therefore periods of slow flight practice should be conducted whilst flying in straight and level, climbing, descending and turning flight. Practising in this manner will give you a greater opportunity to develop your ability and it will also allow you to recognise instinctively any impending stall situation.

Therefore the primary objectives in practising slow flight during the early stage of your aerobatic course will be:

(1) To gain added experience in quickly recognising (through the sense of feel) that the aircraft is very close to the stall.
(2) To develop greater competence and confidence at handling the aircraft during manoeuvres in which very low airspeeds are required.

When you have attained the above objectives you will be able to concentrate more readily upon the aerobatic manoeuvres which are performed during your early aerobatic training.

THE FORCES AND AIRCRAFT CHARACTERISTICS IN SLOW FLIGHT

The amount of lift, and the control of an aircraft in flight depend upon the maintenance of a minimum airspeed. This speed will vary with the all-up weight, imposition of loads due to manoeuvre, aircraft configuration and density altitude. The closer the actual speed to this minimum speed the greater the angle of attack and the less effective are the flying controls.

Figure 14 shows that as the angle of attack increases, the centre of pressure moves forward.

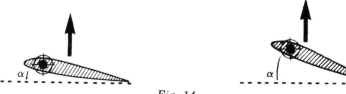

Fig. 14

This movement brings the c.p. and c.g. closer together and weakens the normal nose down tendency brought about by the L/W couple. At the same time the elevators which depend upon the speed of the airflow for their effectiveness will become less responsive as the airspeed reduces with increasing angle of attack.

The ailerons and rudder will also begin to lose their effectiveness as the airspeed decreases and coarse movements of all controls will become necessary to control the aircraft about the three axes. If however the power is increased in a propeller driven aircraft the elevators and rudder will become a little more effective due to the higher speed of the air within the slipstream cylinder. At the low airspeeds associated with slow flight the slipstream effect in producing yaw is very strong and positive use of the rudder must be made to maintain the aircraft in balanced flight. At low speeds and high power settings the larger amount of rudder deflection needed to maintain this balance will produce sufficient further effect to require a positive application of aileron to hold the wings in a laterally level attitude. This will result in the aircraft having to be flown in a 'crossed controls' condition in order to achieve balanced flight with the wings level. Progressing from slow flight to the stall with crossed controls makes the aircraft vulnerable to an emphatic wing drop and possible spin entry.

An important feature in stall training is the development of the ability to estimate the margin of safety above the stalling speed from the diminishing response of the aircraft to movement of the flying controls. Pilots must develop this awareness in order to fly safely at the lower speeds involved during aerobatics.

SETTING UP SLOW FLIGHT

Slow flight should be practised initially from straight and level flight. The power is gradually reduced and the nose attitude raised to maintain a constant altitude. The lateral level, heading and balance must be maintained as the airspeed lowers to a figure of $V_{s1} + 5$ knots. In this situation the aircraft will be flying at the lower end of the power curve (see Fig. 15) and in this region the power available over and above that required for level flight will have deteriorated considerably.

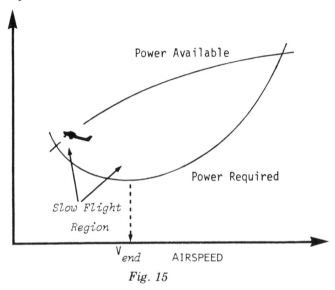

Fig. 15

In these circumstances any attempt to regain lost altitude by raising the nose will result in a rapid increase of induced drag and without additional power the airspeed will lower still further. Little altitude will be gained, and continued raising of the nose will result in altitude being lost and eventually the aircraft will stall. Therefore any attempt to regain altitude when operating at a very low speed demands an increase of power as the nose is raised.

FLIGHT EXERCISE

Your initial revision practice should be carried out at $V_{s1} + 5$ knots. The power should be reduced whilst maintaining straight and level flight. Once the correct power setting has been set to achieve $V_{s1} + 5$ knots the aircraft should be trimmed. Due attention must be paid to lookout and it is advisable not to maintain a constant heading for more than short periods due to the view ahead being obscured by the high nose attitude. A significant effort will need to be made in relation to the maintenance of balance throughout any form of slow flight.

Initially your turns should be limited to 30° of bank and as proficiency increases these should be extended to bank angles of at least 40°. It will be important to increase the power to maintain the airspeed and altitude during level turns at any bank angle.

Descents at slow speed should be practised with and without power. In the power on condition the desired rate of descent can be achieved at the selected airspeed by reducing the power and readjusting the nose attitude to a lower position in the same manner as for a descent during normal flight.

During climbing flight at slow speed the climb performance will be poor due to the increased induced drag and, as seen from the characteristic shape of the horsepower required and horsepower available curves, the aircraft will be operating in an area where a small margin of power available exists (Fig. 15).

Following the practice of slow flight at V_{s1} + 5 knots you should be given the opportunity to practise all normal manoeuvres at the minimum speed at which the aircraft can be controlled.

STALLING

OBJECTIVES

The purpose of including stalling in the aerobatic course is to give you practice at quickly recognising the stall symptoms and to become adjusted to the particular stalling characteristics of the aircraft in use for your aerobatic training. This practice will give you greater confidence at handling the aircraft in stall situations arising from various attitudes and under different load factor conditions.

You will also have the opportunity to improve your stall recovery reactions and this will enable you to respond more quickly and so achieve stall recoveries with a smaller loss of altitude than would otherwise be the case.

An important part of your practice in this exercise will be concerned with recovering from stalls entered during manoeuvres at higher than normal airspeeds. Bearing in mind the unusual attitudes and higher load factors achieved during aerobatic flight, it can be seen that this must be a primary objective in your pre-aerobatic training.

STALLING CHARACTERISTICS

It should first be re-emphasised that a stall can occur at any airspeed, in any attitude and at any power setting. The primary factor which leads to a stall is that the critical angle of attack has been exceeded.

During this stage of your training you will be more concerned with the characteristics of the stall when entered with power on rather than with power off. The stall under these conditions, particularly when load factors greater than one are applied, will usually result in a spirited reaction from the aircraft in terms of a dropping wing and it is therefore advisable to cover this aspect in more depth.

During recoveries from stalls entered under these conditions there is often a very natural tendency for a pilot to use amounts of rudder in excess of that which is reasonably required to prevent further yaw. In this respect it should be understood that the most effective method of preventing a wing dropping further following a stall entry is to move the control column forward and reduce the angle of attack. Providing sufficient forward movement is made, the dropping wing will immediately be arrested and rudder will only be needed to combat further yaw as the aircraft is returned to the required flight attitude. Failure to move the control column sufficiently far forward, for example in an attempt to minimise altitude loss, will result in the wing continuing to drop and a steeply banked attitude may occur.

The above paragraph is a statement of fact and it is not intended to imply that the use of rudder should be ignored at the point of stall or at any time during the recovery. It merely emphasises that if the correct movement of the control column is made then large applications of rudder can be avoided. The importance of appreciating this is the fact that the use of excess rudder during stalls, particularly those entered in a dynamic fashion and with power on, can often lead to a yaw in the opposite direction and the aircraft may snap over into a spin.

On certain aircraft, when the elevators are sufficiently effective at the stall (this will depend upon the centre of gravity position and the amount of power being used) the aircraft can be brought to and held in a stalled condition whereupon it will oscillate from side to side, with first one wing dropping and then the other. The use of rudder whilst the aircraft is in this state can easily result in a sudden spin entry, and your instructor may be able to demonstrate this point to you.

Bearing these facts in mind you should develop an instantaneous reaction at the stall to move the control column forward as a primary action, whilst using just enough rudder to prevent unnecessary yaw.

The aircraft designer can use a variety of methods to reduce the tendency of a wing to drop at the stall. He can for example, use washout, leading edge spoilers on the inboard wing section, wing slats, slots or even arrange to have two different wing sections with different critical angles of attack joined together to make one wing.

On a rectangular wing the airflow separation at the stall usually starts at the root and moves outwards with a further increase in angle of attack. This produces a satisfactory stalling characteristic since only small rolling moments take place, and during power off flight in the clean configuration with a load factor of 1, the effectiveness of the ailerons is retained at the stall. However when the use of a rectangular wing conflicts with other design philosophies or requirements then two different types of wing section having different stalling angles can be combined. The part of the wing with the higher stalling angle is used for the outboard section, and this will result in the inboard section of the wing stalling first and also permit aileron effectiveness (control in roll) to be present at the stall.

Another method is to incorporate washout, which is a design feature providing a twisting of the wing section along its span to produce a smaller angle of incidence at the outboard sections, so that the wing root reaches the stalling angle earlier than the wing tips (Fig. 16). Washout angles are normally of the value of 1° to 3°.

On some aircraft, design requirements favour the use of leading edge spoilers (Fig. 17); these are often called anti-spin or stall strips. They are attached to the leading edges of the inboard wing sections and at high angles of attack disrupt the smooth flow of air and cause the inboard sections to stall before the wing tips.

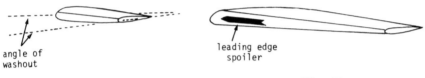

angle of
washout

leading edge
spoiler

Fig. 16

Fig. 17

A further design feature which can reduce the tendency for a wing to drop at the stall is the incorporation of slats or slots. Slats are movable surfaces which can be manually or automatically operated at low speed. Slots perform the same function but are built in as an integral part of the wing. When slats or slots are fitted

slat

along the leading edge section of the wing they will increase the stalling angle of attack of that section of the wing directly behind them and therefore when incorporated along the outboard wing sections they will assist in reducing the stalling speed and also in delaying any tendency for a wing to drop at the stall. Due to the lower stalling speeds achieved when slats or slots are used the controls will be slightly less effective at the stall and will need to be used more positively during stall recovery.

However, although these various features give good results when the aircraft is stalled with power off, a change in the stall characteristics will occur when stalls are entered with power on, and this is particularly so when medium to large amounts of power are being used. The following paragraphs explain why this is so.

At high angles of attack the direction of the thrust line has a significant vertical component as shown in Fig. 18(a). This vertical component of thrust will produce a small increment to the total lift produced by the wing and will therefore reduce the stalling speed by a small amount.

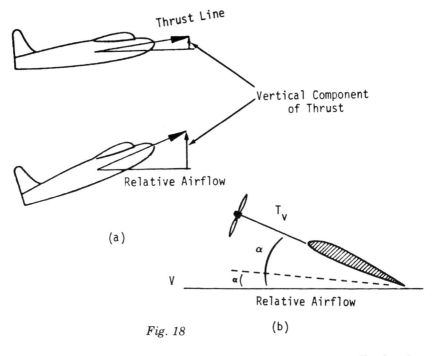

Fig. 18

(b)

The angle of attack of the inboard wing sections will also be modified by the airflow within the slipstream cylinder. In Fig. 18(b) V represents the normal airflow and T_v the airflow produced by the propeller thrust. The resultant of these two airflows is indicated by the dotted line. Since the thrust available with a propeller driven aircraft increases with decrease of speed it is seen that the resultant airflow line will move closer towards the thrust line T_v as power is increased and forward speed decreased.

Therefore the greatest effect of T_v on the normal airflow direction will occur at the stall. When these conditions apply the angle of attack of the wing sections within the slipstream diameter will be decreased and the outboard wing sections may stall first, a condition which is more severe if the flaps are down or when dynamic stall entries are made.

This change in the angle of attack can be quite significant and as a result may overcome the effect of washout or other design features which have been incorporated to prevent the wing tips stalling first.

A further effect of slipstream is the additional energy derived from the increased velocity of airflow over the wing sections behind the propeller. This added energy will produce more lift from the mainplanes and also lead to an increased effectiveness of the tailplane and associated elevator and rudder controls. The ailerons, being outside the slipstream influence will be less effective at the lower stalling speed and control in roll may no longer be possible, and if used under these conditions in fact may produce an adverse yaw leading to autorotation.

A final and adverse effect of slipstream can occur when an aircraft yaws at the stall. Figure 19 shows that due to yaw the propeller slipstream is no longer aligned to the longitudinal axis and as the dynamic pressure in the slipstream is higher than in the free airstream the lift from the starboard wing is greater than from the port wing. However the resultant effect of the slipstream influence is difficult to predict, as the angle of attack and amount of lift variation to each wing will change due to yaw, sideslip angle and slipstream path. The inter-action of these effects could be such that if an aircraft is temporarily held at the stall an oscillatory motion of alternate wing dropping may occur. Whereas this explanation may seem academic it also has a

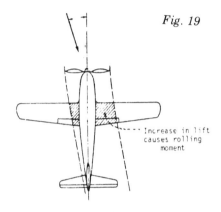

Fig. 19

Increase in lift causes rolling moment

practical implication, in that, if the control column is not moved forward sufficiently to unstall the aircraft, and rudder is used to oppose the initial yaw, the application of rudder could coincide with the moment when the opposite wing drops, thus a flick or similar manoeuvre could be induced leading to a spin entry.

To sum up, if an aircraft is stalled with power on the elevators and rudder will be more effective, but a rapid wing drop may occur which is normally aggravated if a dynamic entry is made. Prompt recovery action will therefore be necessary to prevent the aircraft rolling into an acute bank angle at a time when altitude is also being lost.

Earlier in this section it was emphasised that a stall can occur at any airspeed providing the stalling angle of attack is reached, but as the angle of attack of the wings cannot be observed (unless an angle of attack indicator is fitted) a pilot will have to rely upon other indications. In normal flight conditions when the aircraft is being operated at or near a load factor of one, the basic stalling speed will be a primary indication that the aircraft is nearing a stall condition. However during aerobatic manoeuvres when higher load factors are applied, the pilot will have to rely mainly upon his sense of awareness and judgement of control response to recognise an approach to the stall.

The basic stalling speed of an aircraft means the speed at which the aircraft will stall from level flight with the throttle closed, flaps up and the control column being moved gently back until the stall occurs.

For any particular aircraft the stalling speed will vary according to its all-up weight, the manoeuvre being performed (load factor effect), the amount of power being used and the position of the flaps. These factors are summarised as follows:

The Weight
If extra weight is carried, greater lift will be needed to maintain the aircraft in level flight. Therefore, at all angles of attack including the stalling angle, more airspeed will be needed to provide the greater lift. In other words the stalling speed will be higher.

The Power
When an aircraft has power on the nose attitude will be higher and the stalling speed will be lower. This is because the thrust will be inclined upwards and so contribute to lift. In addition, in propeller driven aircraft the slipstream gives a faster airflow over the wings and helps to prevent the airflow becoming turbulent, as well as providing more lift. The slipstream will also modify the angle of attack of the centre section of the wing.

The Flaps
With the flaps lowered, the lift coefficient of the wings is increased. Therefore the speed required to maintain sufficient lift for level flight is less and the stalling speed is correspondingly reduced. However your training will not normally involve the use of flaps during aerobatic manoeuvres.

The Load Factor
In a turn the lift must be increased in order to maintain level flight, therefore the load factor and the stalling speed will be higher. Sudden accelerations in pitch will also increase the load factor, and this is most noticeable when pulling out of a dive. During this manoeuvre the inertia of the aircraft prevents it from immediately following the flight path suggested by the new attitude, and the angle of attack is thus momentarily increased. This type of manoeuvre can raise the stalling speed considerably.

STALLS AT HIGHER LOAD FACTORS
The type of stalls referred to under this heading are basically manoeuvre stalls, e.g. from turns or pull-ups which during aerobatics are often combined.

You will remember from your basic training that an aircraft can be stalled from a level, descending or climbing turn. Stalls which occur from incorrect handling during a turn, particularly at steeper bank angles, are often dynamic and associated with a positive wing drop when the aircraft is flown with an aft c.g. As with the standard stall recovery the correct procedure to return the aircraft to a normal flight condition will be to move the control column forward and so reduce the angle of attack.

Application of additional power will not have much effect if high power settings are already being used, as in the case of level and climbing steep turns. In the descending steep turn the nose will already be low and application of power will usually only serve to accelerate the aircraft along the downward flight path, leading to an unnecessary loss of altitude.

Rudder should be used in the normal sense to correct for further yaw which in most cases is present during dynamic entries to the stall. The stall characteristics will vary between aircraft and even aircraft of the same type, e.g. differences in location of the c.g., flaps up or down and the amount of power and bank angle used.

Either wing may drop regardless of the direction of turn, but generally a slight sideslip angle predominates just prior to the stall, causing yaw opposite to the direction of turn, and this leads to the higher wing stalling first. Other aspects such as asymmetry of wing or fuselage rigging can however alter this, and the bottom wing can sometimes be the first to stall.

If the predominant yaw is in the direction of the lower wing, e.g. too much bottom rudder being applied, then the inner wing will stall first. If the yaw is in the opposite direction then the outer wing will be the first to stall. In either case recovery is made by a positive forward movement of the control column, by an amount which will only be learned by practice.

Clearly, gross mishandling of the controls will be required to stall an aircraft when the speed is relatively high, because strong aerodynamic forces are involved and more physical effort must be used to bring the aircraft to the stall condition. However, it must also be clearly understood that when the speed is low and the aircraft is at a high angle of attack only a small movement of the control column is required, and due to the lower speed the controls are very light and can easily be moved. This suggests that the most probable reason for an inadvertent stall occurring during a turn is low speed rather than an excessive bank angle.

SECONDARY STALLS

If during the recovery from a stall the control column is not moved forward sufficiently to reduce the angle of attack to below the critical angle, or if you move the control column back too quickly during the final stage of the recovery, a secondary stall will occur.

In this situation the power will have been fully applied and the rearward position of the control column coupled with the pitch up movement due to power will lead to a very sharp stall condition from which the aircraft may yaw and roll rapidly into a state of autorotation leading to a spin. At best, considerable altitude may be lost before further recovery action can be applied.

FLIGHT EXERCISE

AIRMANSHIP

As you will have learned from your basic training the application of airmanship in relation to certain aspects will be vital during stalling practice. Following each stall recovery you will need to re-check that you have sufficient altitude above 3000 ft agl before carrying out further practice. Climbing turns will normally be the best way to regain altitude as by this method you will have the opportunity to search the area, below, above and to either side of the aircraft and so ensure that no other aircraft are in your vicinity. Throughout the exercise you will have to direct your attention to several points of aircraft handling and at the same time keep under constant review the orientation of the aircraft in relation to cloud, ground reference features, and possibly controlled or regulated airspace, etc. Because the airmanship items are many and varied you should continue to use the systematic procedure which you learned during your basic training. The most common form of *aide-mémoire* is the word HASELL and a summary of this procedure is given below:

H. . . Height: sufficient for entry to and recovery from the stall above 3000 ft above ground level. An allowance must be made when the area QNH is used.

A. . . Airframe: as required for the particular stalling practice, e.g. flaps up or down, landing gear position and brakes off (if applicable).

S. . . Security: loose articles stowed, e.g. maps, kneeboards, fire extinguisher secure etc. Harness tight and heading indicator caged (if applicable).

E. . . En route checks and engine considerations: The time spent during individual stall training periods normally occupies from 10 to 20 minutes and it will therefore be necessary to carry out the following checks at intervals – ammeter and suction gauge readings, fuel state and where applicable fuel pressure readings, engine oil temperature and pressure observations and mixture control position etc.

On completion of the stalling exercise the heading indicator should be re-synchronised with the magnetic compass.

L. . . Location: you must ensure that stalls are not carried out over large towns, or in the close vicinity of active airfields or controlled airspace.

L. . . Lookout: a careful lookout must be made before each stall entry and it will be necessary to turn the aircraft to ensure the area all round and below is clear of other air traffic.

Note: When clearing the area it is not essential to carry out continuous turns through 360°. It is however vital to ensure the area in the immediate vicinity and below the aircraft remains clear of other aircraft. To this end, and bearing in mind the need to stay clear of towns, airfields etc., any combination of turn direction and length of turn may be employed.

STALL ENTRY WITH POWER ON

A moderate power setting should be used during the initial stalls but later, as proficiency increases, stalls should be practised at full power. The stall entry and standard recovery action remains unchanged regardless of the power being used, but you will notice the strong tendency for a wing to drop sharply in these circumstances. During power on stalls the slipstream effect at low airspeeds creates a fairly critical condition of unbalance which is not easy to correct and even a momentary yaw at the point of stall is sufficient to cause a wing to drop.

Power on stalls should be practised from level, climbing and turning flight. The entry to the stall should, initially, be fairly gradual and made without rapid control movements or sudden control pressures (accelerated manoeuvre). As your proficiency increases, dynamic stall entries can be practised during turns and pull-ups, and in this way you will have practised stall entries and recoveries in the most likely conditions you will meet during aerobatic manoeuvres.

ENTERING THE STALL DURING NORMAL TURNS

The method of practising a stall and recovery during a turn is to set a low cruising power and enter a normal medium turn. Allow the natural decrease of speed to occur and then gently raise the nose to decrease the speed still further (a slight increase in bank may be used to assist the speed to decrease). At this stage, and whilst maintaining the bank angle, ease the control column back in one continuous movement until the aircraft stalls. This backward movement of the control column should be positive but not violent.

During a turn a wing will normally drop at the point of stall and becomes the most easily recognised stall feature. An immediate unstalling of the wings will be achieved by a positive forward movement of the control column. The elevators, ailerons and rudder are then used in the normal way to complete the recovery and return the aircraft to straight and level flight.

ENTERING THE STALL DURING A STEEP TURN
Having completed the safety checks the aircraft should be placed in a steep turn and the increase of power delayed until the speed is below 1.5 the V_{s1}. At this stage the back pressure should be increased whilst maintaining the bank angle. The backward movement of the control column should continue without hesitation until the aircraft stalls.

At the stall some buffet may be felt and one wing will usually tend to drop; the rapidity of this wing drop action will depend upon the type of aircraft, the position of the c.g., and the amount of bank at the time of the stall.

THE RECOVERY
Recovery at the incipient stage is easily effected by relaxing the back pressure on the control column and either continuing with the turn or returning to the level attitude. Recovery from the developed stall follows the same lines, but a positive forward pressure on the control column will be required or the aircraft may be slow to recover, and during this period a wing drop can be very rapid and could result in the aircraft becoming inverted.

Rudder is used to stop further yaw, and the power adjusted as applicable depending upon the nose attitude in pitch at the time of the recovery action.

SPINNING

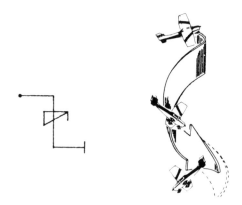

INTRODUCTION

The objective of spin training in the current Private Pilot Licence course is to teach a pilot how to recognise this situation at the incipient stage and to instinctively recover before a developed spin occurs.

If the aircraft used in your basic training was cleared for deliberate spins, however, your instructor may have given you the opportunity to practise entry into and recovery from a full spin. Nonetheless it will be necessary to become acquainted with the aircraft's spinning characteristics in more detail during your aerobatic course.

OBJECTIVES

During the execution of aerobatic manoeuvres the aircraft will often be flown in situations which are conducive to inadvertent spin entries. Therefore it is necessary that you reinforce your proficiency to recover at the incipient stage, but because of the greater risk of entering a developed spin the procedure for entry and recovery from a full spin must be demonstrated and practised until you are completely proficient at recovering from this manoeuvre.

AIRCRAFT RESTRICTIONS

Before the practice of developed spins in any aircraft you must determine that the aircraft is cleared to perform the manoeuvre and also whether any specific limitations apply, e.g. whether the number of turns in a spin are limited, whether inverted spins are allowed, etc.

Normally an aircraft on the UK register which is cleared for performing aerobatics will also be cleared for intentional spinning. However you must bear in mind that variations may occur between different aircraft and even aircraft of the same type and you should abide by four simple rules before carrying out developed spins. These are:

(1) If the aircraft Flight/Owner's Manual/Pilot's Operating Handbook states that spinning is prohibited the issue is clear cut – under no circumstances attempt to place the aircraft into a spin.

(2) If the aircraft Flight/Owner's Manual/Pilot's Operating Handbook contains restrictions relating to spinning you must obey them.

(3) The method of spin recovery as contained in the Aircraft Manual must be followed, unless the UK Airworthiness Supplement states otherwise.

(4) If no information is available regarding spinning on the specific aircraft type – do not carry out intentional spins.

THE DEVELOPED SPIN

This is a condition of stalled flight during which the aircraft also describes a spiral descent. The aircraft will be simultaneously rolling, yawing and pitching until recovery is initiated by the pilot.

The cause of the spin may be deliberate or inadvertent but in any case it will develop into a condition of autorotation.

Autorotation

Figure 20 illustrates the aerodynamic characteristics in relation to the C_L and C_D curves versus the angle of attack for a typical light aircraft during the fully developed autorotative stage.

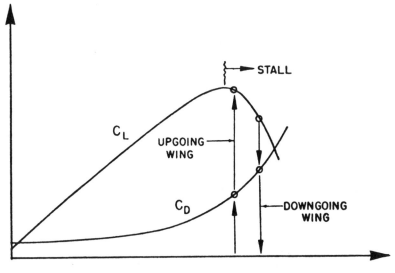

Fig. 20 α ANGLE OF ATTACK α_L α_R

The downgoing wing being more stalled will produce more drag causing the aircraft to yaw in the direction of the downgoing wing. Due to the upgoing wing being less stalled, it will always have more lift than the downgoing wing and this action will be self perpetuating, hence the term 'autorotation'.

Spin Characteristics

During a spin, the aircraft will lose altitude rapidly and descend along a vertical path about the spin axis, the helix of which is fairly small and can be less than the span of the wings. An important characteristic during a spin is that the predominant tendency is to continue the autorotation and the aircraft generally has a spinning motion which is primarily rolling, but with moderate yaw and a degree of sideslip. If an aircraft has a large amount of directional stability, this will have a favourable influence on the spin characteristics as it will minimise the displacement due to yaw and make it easier to effect a recovery.

The actual motion of an aeroplane and its path through the air during a spin manoeuvre depend upon many complex aerodynamic considerations which involve inertia forces and moments. Nevertheless, there are certain basic facts which relate to spins and with which all pilots should be familiar.

The development and the characteristics of a spin will depend upon the aircraft design and the distribution of its mass, as well as the operation of the control surfaces. The aircraft will usually rotate several times before it settles down into the state of spinning steadily and the pitch angle it takes up may be steep or flat, the latter characteristic being significantly affected by the position of the centre of gravity.

The actual motions of the aircraft throughout the entry to, and during a spin, are of a complex nature. Once the aircraft has settled into a spin, the forces and moments acting upon it will be in equilibrium, and this balance of forces and moments will determine the values of angle of attack, sideslip, turn radius, rate of descent and other factors.

During the steady spin, the aircraft will be in a condition where the rate of yaw and roll will settle down to a constant value and the rate of descent will also stabilise. Some aircraft, because of design features, or the position of the centre of gravity may be unable to achieve a true spin, and as a result, the forces and moments will not balance out. In this case an oscillatory spin motion will occur which could more accurately be described as an autorotative spiral.

During a settled spin, it is the balance of the moments which will determine the final state of equilibrium and which will have a large influence upon the recovery characteristics. The actual balance of the forces is of less importance, but in view of their effect upon the rate of descent and the considerations relating to the position of the centre of gravity, they must be discussed here. The three primary forces are the resultant of the aerodynamic forces, the inertia forces (considered as centrifugal forces) and the weight, and these forces interact approximately as shown in Fig. 21.

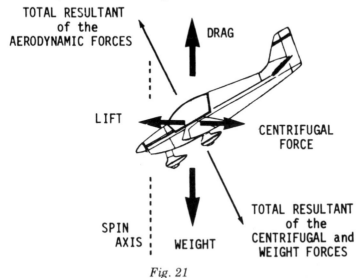

Fig. 21

The position and direction of weight is easily established as acting directly downward through the centre of gravity, and as throughout the spin, the aircraft will be descending the overall relative airflow will therefore be coming from below. In consequence, the vertical component of the resultant of the aerodynamic forces labelled drag in Fig. 21, will be acting against the weight and at a certain rate of descent will balance the weight, i.e. in a steady spin the rate of descent will settle to a constant value.

Lift acting at 90° to the overall relative airflow will now be approximately horizontal, and the centrifugal force brought about by the aircraft rotation in the spin will oppose the lift. The conditions for equilibrium will be met when drag = weight and lift = centrifugal force.

Figure 22 shows the resultant of the aerodynamic forces, the effect of up elevator and the direction of the centrifugal forces in relation to the centre of gravity.

A = aerodynamic force (resultant of lift and drag)
B = aerodynamic effect of 'up elevator'
C, D are inertia or centrifugal forces arising due to the distribution of mass.

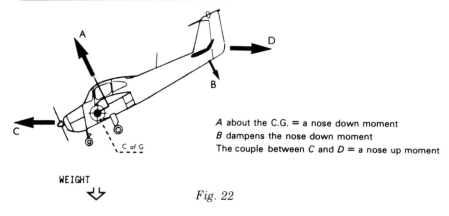

A about the C.G. = a nose down moment
B dampens the nose down moment
The couple between C and D = a nose up moment

WEIGHT

Fig. 22

The aerodynamic resultant A of lift and drag acting behind the centre of gravity produces a nose down moment and the up elevator force tends to oppose this. The centrifugal forces acting on the fore and aft masses of the aircraft will produce a nose up moment. It can, therefore, be seen that the closer the centre of gravity is to the aerodynamic force, the flatter the spin will become. This may be more clearly visualised if one considers the effect of having the centre of gravity aft of the aerodynamic force, in which case, both the aerodynamic force and the centrifugal forces will be acting together to flatten the spin.

If the spin flattens, the angle of attack increases and the resulting increase of drag will decrease the rate of descent. The moment due to the centrifugal forces will have a stronger effect in the horizontal plane, which will lead to a decrease in the spin radius and an increase in the rate of rotation.

EFFECT OF THE CENTRE OF GRAVITY ON SPINNING CHARACTERISTICS

The spinning characteristics of any particular aircraft will vary with the position of the centre of gravity, even though its position is within the permitted limits for the aircraft concerned. The effect of a forward position of the centre of gravity is to cause a steeper spin with a faster rate of descent. However, recovery action is easier as the spin is far less stable. An extreme forward position of the centre of gravity may in some cases prevent a spin being achieved altogether, in which case, the aircraft will remain in a steep, and usually tight, spiral descent, during which the airspeed increases.

The effect of an aft centre of gravity is to make the spin flatter, in which case, the rate of descent is less, the spin is more stable, and recovery is more difficult. If the centre of gravity is aft of the permitted limits, a serious situation can occur where the aircraft may not be capable of recovering from a settled spin condition.

EFFECT OF AIRCRAFT INERTIA UPON SPIN RECOVERY CHARACTERISTICS

The ratio of pitching, rolling and yawing inertia may vary in different aircraft and will affect the spin recovery characteristics and the part that using ailerons will play in spin recovery. Therefore, reference to the particular aircraft manual must be made to ascertain the correct use of the controls during spin recovery.

THE SPIRAL DIVE

This condition can be entered from a stalled or semi-stalled configuration in which the nose of the aircraft lowers rapidly during the period in which the wings are rolling into a steeply banked attitude. This condition is also one which can be reached during a steeply banked turn if the nose is allowed to drop too low. Once the aircraft has adopted this attitude the airspeed will increase rapidly and applying back pressure to the control column will only serve to worsen the situation as the turn will tighten thereby causing the nose to drop further, leading to the possibility of overstressing the airframe.

The correct recovery action is to close the throttle completely and positively roll the wings level, following this the aircraft can be eased out of the dive. When levelling the wings it must be appreciated that at the greater speeds associated with the spiral dive condition, the pilot will need to apply higher than normal control forces to the ailerons in order to roll the wings level.

RECOVERY FROM AN INVERTED SPIN

In the event of inadvertently entering an inverted spin during aerobatics it must be appreciated that the direction of roll and the direction of yaw are opposite to each other. The direction of spin will nevertheless be indicated by the turn indicator and full opposite rudder should be used against this indication. Following this action the control column should be moved smoothly rearwards until the spin stops, upon which a recovery should be made to the nearest horizon and if necessary a roll out to erect flight can then be executed.

THE PRECISION RECOVERY FROM THE DEVELOPED SPIN

Most pilots will have made a brief encounter with spinning during their PPL training. However the method of entry and normal exit may well have not been of the type to achieve a satisfactory competition spin. Since spinning is wasteful in terms of height, the 1, $1\frac{1}{4}$, $1\frac{1}{2}$ or $1\frac{3}{4}$ turn spin is likely to be the longest used in an aerobatic contest.

A spin is defined as autorotation in a stalled condition, entered from level flight at $1g$ and the exit line during competition aerobatics should be a brief vertical descent prior to level flight. To achieve the required entry with modern aircraft it may be found necessary to use a small amount of power (if permitted by the flight manual), and as the aircraft decelerates to V_{s1} + 10 knots the rudder should be fully and smoothly deflected. As the rudder reaches the maximum stop the control column or wheel should be smoothly and firmly pulled to the full aft position. Any power used during the entry should now be eliminated by closing the throttle.

By using a line feature and reference points the number of turns must be counted off in $\frac{1}{2}$ units. In the early phase of training, recovery action in the form laid down in the aircraft manual should be taken after one complete turn, and the further rotational deviation of the aircraft in the recovery noted. This amount can then be used to ensure that in future spins, recovery can be effected exactly on the required line.

Compared with the typical PPL training spin where most aircraft recover in a pitch attitude of 45° to 60° nose down the competition spin has a vertical exit line. This means that rather more forward movement of the control column or wheel is required to establish the vertical. As soon as this has been achieved the aircraft should be firmly but smoothly levelled before the airspeed accelerates to an unacceptable level. Disorientation can be minimised by looking up as much as possible to pick out the reference line rather than gazing directly forward over the engine cowling.

FLIGHT EXERCISE

When the safety checks have been completed the usual method of spin entry from the level flight attitude will be to reduce the power to a low or idle setting and raise the nose slightly to reduce the airspeed. Maintain the aircraft in balance with the wings level and continue moving the control column back until the aircraft is near or at the stall.

At this stage whilst holding the wings level, apply full rudder smoothly and positively towards the required spin direction and move the control column fully back. The aircraft will now yaw and roll into the direction of applied rudder, autorotation will occur and the spin will develop. The controls will have to be maintained in the direction they have been applied and the control column will need to be held fully back. Maintain a visual reference outside the cockpit during the first few practice spins and thereafter the habit of checking the turn indicator should be added to confirm the spin direction.

Some aircraft, notably those with a forward c.g., are reluctant to enter a spin unless the conditions are right and the timing of the control movements is correct. In this respect it should be appreciated that the ailerons should be used as required to hold the wings level up to the moment of rudder application, and any movement of the control column in the direction of spin, i.e. towards the lowering wing must be avoided or the applied yaw will be reduced.

An entry to the spin can be made from many flight attitudes, e.g. level, climbing, descending, etc., but many modern light training aircraft, due to their forward c.g., reduced rudder area, and limited up elevator movement, often give difficulties in producing clean and positive spin entries from a power off condition. With power on, spin entries are easier and more positive and do not require as much control force as entries with power off. Therefore spin entries may more easily be achieved by using 1400 to 1500 RPM during the entry stage as this will provide greater rudder and elevator effectiveness. However it will be necessary to establish whether power on entries to deliberate spins are permitted for the particular aircraft before using this method.

During the deliberate spin entered as a training exercise the direction of spin will automatically be known but in an inadvertent spin the direction will have to be established before correct recovery action can be taken. During the training spins the direction of the rotation of the aircraft can be seen with reference to the ground. However if an inadvertent spin should ever occur visual reference of this sort could be inconclusive in determining the spin direction, and a more precise method will become necessary.

This can be achieved by reference to the turn indicator. As the direction of spin is determined by the direction of yaw, the turn indicator will indicate a turn in the same direction as the yaw. Therefore during a spin to the left the turn indicator will show a turn to the left, and when spinning to the right a right turn will be indicated by the turn indicator.

The degree of turn indicated during the spin is not necessarily the maximum, and dependent upon the stage of spin, could be less than that shown whilst executing turns during taxying. The balance portion of the instrument, whether it is a ball or needle type of presentation will not be of any value in determining spin direction and the same applies to the attitude and heading indicators either of which could have toppled or in any event be confusing to interpret. To sum up therefore, these last instrument indications cannot be used with sufficient accuracy to determine the direction in which an aircraft is spinning.

THE SPIN RECOVERY

The exact recovery procedure will be contained in the manual for the specific aircraft type, however there are some general points which will apply to many aircraft. These are the use of rudder, and the need to close the throttle if the spin has been entered with power on. The rudder is the primary anti-yaw control and therefore during a developed spin it is usual to apply rudder opposite to the direction of spin before moving the elevators. The use of power with its slipstream effect in the case of propeller driven aircraft, is usually unhelpful to recovery and the throttle should be closed without delay.

A basic spin recovery which has been used over the years is given below but it must be stressed that the recommendations contained in the aircraft manual in connection with spin recovery must be used for the specific aircraft type.

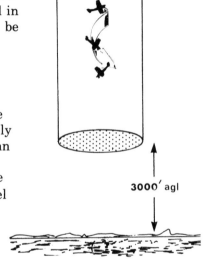

3000′ agl

- Throttle closed.
- Determine spin direction.
- Ailerons held neutral.
- Apply full rudder opposite to the spin direction: pause momentarily and then ease the control column forward until the spin stops.
- When the spin stops centralise the rudder and use the ailerons to level the wings. Once the wings are approximately level ease the aircraft out of the dive.

SPINNING FROM THE TURN

The most probable reason for an inadvertent spin during an advanced turn is lack of attention to airspeed, or gross over-controlling of the aircraft. The former is more likely under normal conditions. To avoid large stresses being imposed on the aircraft structure by the pilot during practice it is advisable to reduce speed during the turn and make the spin entry below 1.5 the V_{s1}.

Note: Not all the aircraft are cleared for practice spin entries with power on, therefore it will be necessary to carefully check the aircraft manual to see whether any spin restrictions of this nature apply.

Once the safety checks have been completed and the steep turn initiated the spin entry may be set up by reducing the speed until the onset of aerodynamic or artificial stall warning, at which point whilst continuing to increase the angle of attack the rudder should be smoothly and fully deflected in the direction of the desired spin. Due to the added effectiveness of the elevators and rudder when relatively high power is used, the controls will require a smaller movement to produce spin entry than when the aircraft is flown at lower speeds and low or idle power.

A return to normal flight is effected by the use of the spin recovery as applicable for the aircraft type but especial care must be used to close the throttle, as the entry from a climbing or level turn will have been executed with a relatively high power setting. Apart from the increased autorotative forces involved, leaving the power on for even a short period during a spin manoeuvre will usually lead to a rapid rise in airspeed and consequently a greater altitude loss. Alternatively in many aircraft the use of power during a spin will tend to flatten the pitch attitude and cause a delayed spin recovery.

SPIN RECOVERY AT THE INCIPIENT STAGE

Review and practice (as necessary) of recovering from spins at the incipient stage will be included in your course of aerobatic training. The practice should cover spin situations entered under different conditions and from various flight attitudes.

THE LAZY 8

This manoeuvre is given its name because whilst performing it the aircraft's extended longitudinal axis is made to trace a pattern in the shape of an 8 lying on its side. The manoeuvre requires a pilot to apply constantly changing control pressures due to its combination of climbing and descending turns at varying airspeeds.

OBJECTIVES

The main purpose is to improve a pilot's co-ordination by creating the need for varying control forces in different directions in order to accurately control the aircraft's flight path to produce the lazy 8 pattern. Proficiency in the performance of lazy 8s will develop a pilot's skill in maintaining balanced flight throughout a sequence of changing attitudes in pitch and roll with a continuously varying airspeed.

THE FLIGHT MANOEUVRE

This basically consists of two 180° turns in opposite directions whilst performing a climb and descent in a symmetrical pattern during each of the turns. The only time that the wings will be laterally level is at that moment when the bank is being reversed on completion of each 180° change in heading (see Fig. 23). A distant reference point should be chosen (upwind or downwind) as a base for positioning the aircraft throughout the manoeuvre. This point should preferably be on the horizon although a convenient cloud just above the horizon will do if a suitable ground feature is not available. The manoeuvre is commenced from level flight at the manufacturers' recommended airspeed and with the chosen reference point at 90° to the pilot's line of sight along the wing (Fig. 24).

Note: It is preferable to choose the reference point so that the entry heading is crosswind and so prevent the aircraft being drifted unnecessarily far downwind during the performance of the manoeuvres.

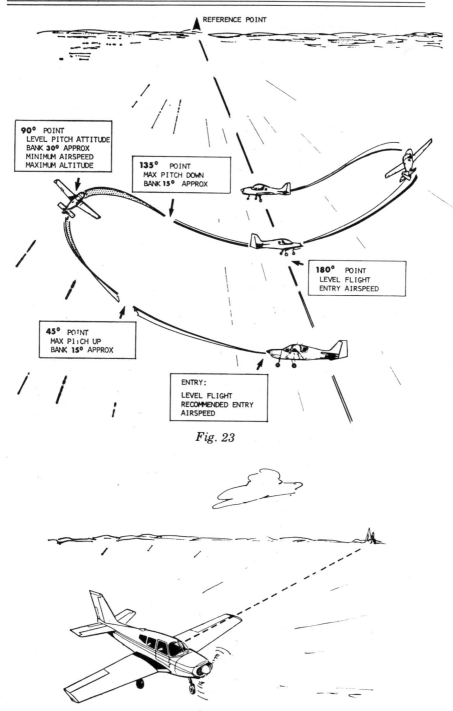

REFERENCE POINT

90° POINT
LEVEL PITCH ATTITUDE
BANK 30° APPROX
MINIMUM AIRSPEED
MAXIMUM ALTITUDE

135° POINT
MAX PITCH DOWN
BANK 15° APPROX

180° POINT
LEVEL FLIGHT
ENTRY AIRSPEED

45° POINT
MAX PITCH UP
BANK 15° APPROX

ENTRY:
LEVEL FLIGHT
RECOMMENDED ENTRY
AIRSPEED

Fig. 23

Fig. 24

FLIGHT EXERCISE

First ensure that the area is clear of other aircraft and then take up a heading which is at 90° to the reference point. When this point is abeam the wing tip a gradually banked climbing turn is initiated towards the reference point. The climbing turn must be controlled in a manner which brings the aircraft to the highest pitch attitude after 45° of turn. During this portion of the manoeuvre the angle of bank will be gradually increasing and the airspeed will be decreasing. Unless the manoeuvre is begun with a slow rate of roll, the combination of increasing pitch and bank will cause the rate of turn to be too rapid and the 45° reference point will be reached before the highest pitch attitude has been attained.

From the 45° point to the 90° point of the turn the bank angle is gradually increased so that at the 90° point the bank should be approximately 30° and the airspeed at its minimum. Providing the correct control movement timing is being used at this stage, the airspeed will still be decreasing as the bank is increased to 30°. Therefore a slight amount of opposite aileron pressure will normally have to be applied to prevent the bank from becoming too steep. On passing the 45° point the nose of the aircraft is allowed to pitch down slowly towards the horizon and through the 90° reference point. It is at this stage, whilst the nose is pitching down that an imaginary line from the pilot's eyes and parallel to the longitudinal axis of the aircraft should pass through the 90° reference point, i.e. the aircraft's nose will appear to slide down through the reference point on its way to the 135° position of the manoeuvre.

After passing through the 90° reference point the aircraft should continue in a descending turn whilst the bank angle is gradually reduced so that at the 135° point the angle of bank is approximately 15°. At this point the nose of the aircraft will be in its lowest pitch attitude for the manoeuvre and the airspeed will be increasing.

From the 135° position the change in the angle of bank and pitch attitude must be co-ordinated so that the aircraft arrives at the 180° point in level flight and at the airspeed used at the commencement.

Upon reaching the 180° point an immediate climbing turn in the opposite direction must be commenced.

Throughout the whole manoeuvre particular attention will need to be made to the need for changing the pressure on the rudder pedals in order to maintain the aircraft in balance. The correct power setting for the performance of lazy 8s is one which will maintain the altitude for the maximum and minimum airspeeds used during the climb and descent phase of the manoeuvre. One object being to attain the same altitude at the commencement and completion of the 8.

THE CHANDELLE

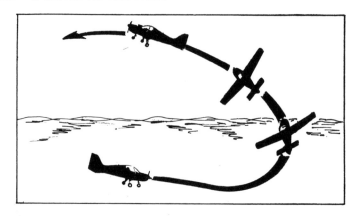

Basically a chandelle consists of a climbing turn commencing from straight and level flight and finishing when the aircraft has been turned through 180°. On the completion of the manoeuvre the aircraft wings should be level with the nose in a high pitch attitude at the minimum controllable airspeed.

OBJECTIVES

To give the pilot the opportunity to develop a high degree of co-ordination and orientation. This will require planning, and a feel for maximum performance flight by using control techniques at varying airspeeds and attitudes. This must be achieved in bank and pitch, whilst the aircraft gains the maximum altitude consistent with the bank angles and power settings used.

THE FLIGHT MANOEUVRE

A distant reference point should be chosen, preferably upwind or downwind so that the manoeuvre is accomplished across wind in order to prevent the aircraft drifting too far downwind during a continued sequence. The chandelle is commenced from approximately level flight (a slight dive may have to be used to obtain the recommended entry airspeed). As the aircraft wing tip becomes abeam the selected reference point a co-ordinated turn in the direction of the reference point is commenced. The bank angle will normally be 30°. After the turn has been established it should immediately be converted into a climbing turn, and one which attains the highest pitch attitude as the nose reaches the 90° position. Power can be increased as appropriate but its application should be smooth and gradual.

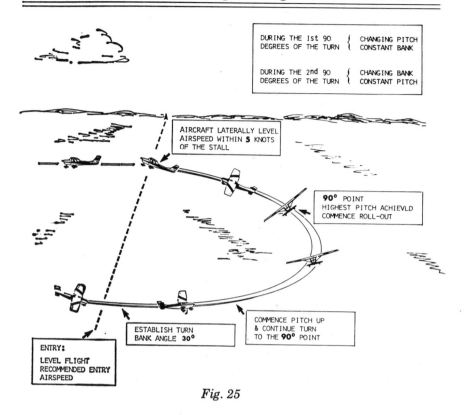

DURING THE 1st 90 DEGREES OF THE TURN { CHANGING PITCH / CONSTANT BANK

DURING THE 2nd 90 DEGREES OF THE TURN { CHANGING BANK / CONSTANT PITCH

AIRCRAFT LATERALLY LEVEL
AIRSPEED WITHIN 5 KNOTS
OF THE STALL

90° POINT
HIGHEST PITCH ACHIEVLD
COMMENCE ROLL-OUT

ESTABLISH TURN
BANK ANGLE 30°

COMMENCE PITCH UP
& CONTINUE TURN
TO THE 90° POINT

ENTRY:
LEVEL FLIGHT
RECOMMENDED ENTRY
AIRSPEED

Fig. 25

The angle of bank should remain constant until the aircraft has reached the 90° position. Thereafter the bank is gradually reduced so that the wings are level at the 180° point. The pitch attitude should remain constant from the 90° position until the 180° point. Thus the manoeuvre will be completed when the aircraft has turned through 180° and is flying at the minimum controllable airspeed. After momentarily holding a constant heading in this attitude the aircraft should be returned to normal straight and level flight, following which a chandelle in the opposite direction can be entered.

During the manoeuvre the airspeed is constantly decreasing, therefore during a chandelle to the left (propeller rotation clockwise) the rudder pressure must be constantly increased to maintain the aircraft in a balanced condition. Throughout the whole manoeuvre the pilot will have to divide his attention between flying the aircraft accurately and achieving the correct orientation in relation to the entry and exit headings.

RECOVERIES FROM UNUSUAL ATTITUDES

INTRODUCTION

During your basic training for a Private Pilot's Licence you were introduced to and required to practise recoveries from certain unusual attitudes. These concerned a steep bank angle in combination with a high or low nose attitude and formed the typical situations which you might get into during normal flying operations. However during the practice of aerobatic manoeuvres the unusual attitudes which occur will often be more extreme and associated with a near vertical or vertical attitude and also inverted flight.

OBJECTIVES

The teaching of recovery from these marked extremes of attitudes will be an essential part of your training so that you become proficient at returning the aircraft to a normal flight situation in the event of a manoeuvre not going as planned and resulting in the aircraft assuming a vertical or inverted attitude.

UNUSUAL ATTITUDES

Basically there are two types of unusual attitude taught during training; one where the aircraft nose is high and one where it is low. These attitudes are normally considered with Advanced Turns so it can be assumed for the purpose of the following recovery procedures that a steep bank angle is present in either case.

RECOVERY PROCEDURES

If the nose is high and the bank is steep:

● Ease forward on the control column and increase power smoothly whilst rolling the wings level through the use of aileron and rudder.

● Care must be used to handle all controls gently as the aircraft may be in the region of the stall.

If the nose is low and the bank is steep:

The recovery from this condition is similar to the recovery from a spiral dive.

● Reduce the power.

● Use aileron and rudder to roll the wings level and then recover from the dive in the normal way.

If at any time the aircraft inadvertently reaches a vertical or near vertical nose up attitude with the airspeed extremely low and insufficient control remaining to continue the manoeuvre through a looping phase, any mishandling of the situation at this point can cause an entry into a spin or a hammerhead stall. Spins will have been practised and should therefore not present a problem providing sufficient altitude is available for the recovery. In the event that the aircraft has run out of airspeed in the near vertical nose up attitude a tail slide may occur and this can lead to severe stresses being applied to the airframe and rear control surfaces. In this situation, it will be extremely important to hold the control column central and either wait for the nose to drop of its own accord or to apply pressure on the left rudder (propeller rotation clockwise) to help the aircraft yaw to the left and encourage the nose to drop sideways. Left rudder applied when power is being used will assist the normal torque and slipstream effect and by this means a whip stall or hammerhead may be avoided.

In the event that the aircraft has inadvertently become inverted with insufficient airspeed for the ailerons to be effective it will be advisable to move the control column backwards to lower the nose and when sufficient airspeed has been regained a roll out to the upright (erect) position can be made. It is normally better to 'half roll' out of this situation rather than attempt a pull through which will invariably result in a greater loss of altitude and may also cause the airspeed to exceed the V_{ne}.

FLIGHT EXERCISE

This will initially take the form of revision of previous practice in recovering from attitudes in which the bank is steep and the nose of the aircraft is pitched well up or well down.

Recoveries from the near vertical attitude will follow, but the true vertical attitude will be avoided by your instructor as considerable stress can be imposed on the airframe if a whip stall occurs during this type of practice.

Recoveries from the inverted position will be introduced before you commence solo practice in rolling manoeuvres.

Restarting an engine in-flight

During the extremes of attitude which are associated with performing aerobatic manoeuvres, there will always be an added risk of the engine stopping when the airspeed is very low and power has been reduced to an idle or near idle setting. The possibility of this occurring must be anticipated and providing sufficient altitude is available this situation should not be hazardous. Most aircraft manuals outline the procedure to be followed for starting the engine in-flight and these procedures should be carefully learned and followed.

Modern training aircraft use battery operated starting systems and these work just as efficiently in the air as on the ground. However, in the case of older aircraft without self starters it may be necessary to start the engine by diving to turn the propeller. In this case the engine controls should be set in the normal positiion for a ground start, the ignition should be checked in the 'ON' position and this also applies to the fuel selector. In most cases a steep diving attitude will be necessary to ensure the engine starts early in the dive so avoiding losing unnecessary altitude, which in any case may be considerable. Whilst on the subject of altitude it must be stressed that attempts to re-start the engine should not be continued to the detriment of planning and executing a safe forced landing.

It is worth mentioning at this stage that engines may fail not only because of aerobatic manoeuvres but also through lack of fuel, incorrect mixture, etc., so it is always very important to carry out the normal engine pre-starting checks and thus confirm if the engine has stopped solely as a result of mishandling an aerobatic manoeuvre.

The Basic Aerobatic Manoeuvres

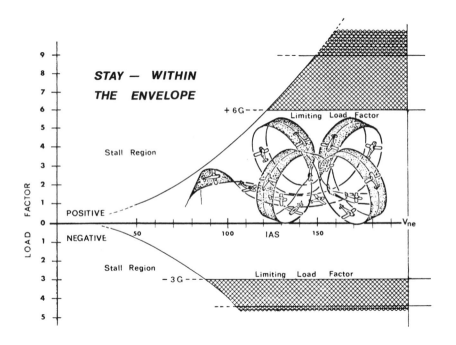

The Basic Aerobatic Manoeuvres

INTRODUCTION

Pilots and instructors tend to have subtle differences in their techniques of executing aerobatic manoeuvres and it should be borne in mind that in all forms of instruction it is perfectly acceptable for different methods to be used to achieve the same result. Therefore you must appreciate that your instructor may use slight variations in techniques to those which are outlined on the following pages.

Additionally, it should also be understood that individual aircraft often have different flight characteristics, particularly in relation to the effect of the rate and amount of control movements. It is therefore difficult to write a detailed explanation of exactly how an aerobatic manoeuvre can best be performed which applies to all types of aircraft.

Because of these considerations and the fact that the following manoeuvres are covered in a manner which is slanted towards competition style manoeuvres your instruction may, to some degree, vary from the actual way the manoeuvre is performed in this manual.

You will also have to bear in mind that when flying a different aircraft to that used in your aerobatic training you will have to spend a little time getting accustomed to its handling characteristics before being able to perform aerobatic manoeuvres as skilfully as those which you were able to accomplish in your training aircraft. Should the aircraft be a two seater, then a checkout with a qualified aerobatic instructor should be considered. In the event that a single seater aircraft is used a thorough briefing from a qualified instructor should be obtained.

THE LOOP

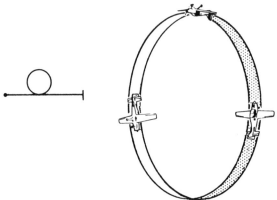

INTRODUCTION

Practice of any of the basic aerobatic manoeuvres should, initially, be limited in length and it will be more beneficial to carry out regular short periods of practice rather than concentrated periods at irregular intervals.

The accelerated manoeuvre stall (*g* stall) will be the type which can be met with most commonly during looping manoeuvres. You should therefore bear in mind that this is not necessarily a 'high speed' stall in the strict sense of having a high airspeed. It merely means that regardless of airspeed, if the control column is moved back too far and too quickly the stalling angle of attack can be exceeded and a stall will occur at a speed higher than the aircraft's basic stalling speed. For example, a too vigorous 'pull up' into a loop could cause the aircraft to stall at a relatively high airspeed, but equally, if the control column is moved back too far when approaching the top (slow speed) section of a loop the same type of stall will occur but in this case at a low airspeed (see Fig. 26).

Your recent revision in practising stalling should allow you to recognise the onset of this type of stall and you must appreciate that the amount of forward pressure needed on the control column to recover will vary from a slight relaxation of back pressure to a positive push forward depending upon the degree of stall and how quickly recovery action is taken.

THE FLIGHT MANOEUVRE

The loop basically consists of a 360° turn in the vertical plane, during which the wings are kept laterally level. The aircraft should remain in balance, and a positive load factor (which varies in amount) be applied throughout.

Fig. 26

The loop is entered at the speed recommended in the aircraft manual and in most light aircraft an initial dive will be necessary to achieve this speed. Co-ordination of all control movements, including the throttle, will be an essential part of the manoeuvre, but during the very early stages of your practice the instructor may lighten your workload in one or two ways. For example, in the case of aircraft fitted with a fixed pitch propeller he may ask you to set the throttle at a particular RPM and then leave it alone during the initial dive. This setting will be one which he knows will be close to, but will not exceed the maximum allowable RPM by the time the recommended entry speed has been attained.

Again, your instructor may ignore the consideration of selecting a ground reference feature and asking you to maintain orientation in relation to it during the manoeuvre, until you have had the opportunity of getting the aircraft round the loop and becoming adjusted to the control pressures and *g* forces involved. Some instructors may even ask you to remove your feet from the rudder pedals during the first few loops which you make. This is to avoid you over-correcting for yaw during the marked changes of airspeed which occur throughout the manoeuvre. This type of fault is fairly common and also aggravates the difficulty of keeping the wings laterally level over the top portion of the loop when the horizon is no longer visible.

Bearing these variations in instructional technique in mind, the eventual and correct sequence will be as follows; having completed the safety checks, selected a reference line feature and established that the area is clear of other aircraft the initial dive is commenced to obtain the entry speed. Both the airspeed indicator and the tachometer will have to be monitored during the dive, the latter to ensure that the RPM do not exceed the red line.

Upon reaching the entry speed a positive and smooth back pressure is applied and as the nose comes up above the horizon with airspeed reducing, increase the power to maximum again taking care not to exceed the red line figure. A positive check should be made to level the wings as the nose passes through the horizon and rudder should be used to maintain the aircraft in balance. The ability to keep the wings laterally level and the aircraft in balance will only come with practice and after you have carried out several loops you should be able to occasionally glance at the balance indicator to assist in achieving balance.

Remember that the further effect of yaw is roll, therefore if you have to use rudder to centre the ball you will also have to move the control column slightly to counteract this further effect and keep the wings level.

In the loop the greatest *g* force will be during the initial 'pull-up' and the pull through from the vertical to level flight in the final part of the manoeuvre. The lightest (but still positive) *g* will occur over the top section when the aircraft is inverted. The main consideration in relation to *g* during your early practice is that you must maintain a positive pressure between yourself and the aircraft seat all the way round the loop. In the ideal sense this will necessitate a gradual and continuous backward movement of the control column until you have passed the top section, after which you will need to graduate your control pressure compatible with the rising airspeed as you descend through the vertical and the final pull through into level flight.

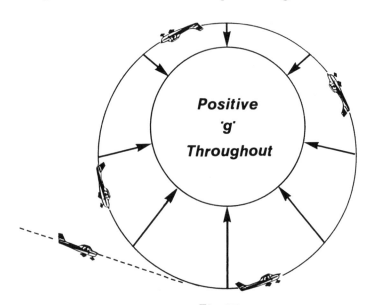

Fig. 27

It must also be pointed out that the timing involved in the rate of pull, or the rate at which you relax back pressure on the control column will inevitably vary due to the effects of human imprecision in the handling of the aircraft controls as the aircraft proceeds through the loop. Ultimately the degree of smoothness and accuracy which is achieved will depend upon the amount of practice obtained by the pilot.

During the inverted portion of the loop the airspeed will be very low and care must be used to avoid any sudden back pressure which could easily lead to a stall, possibly followed by a rapid rolling action. As the nose commences to move down towards the horizon you will need to look well ahead and through the top section of the windshield or through the skylight windows or perspex canopy, in order to see the horizon as soon as possible and so make any correction needed to level the wings.

After the nose has passed through the horizon the throttle setting should be smoothly reduced to avoid exceeding the limiting RPM during the dive. It should be noted that in the interests of engine handling the throttle should not be completely closed at this stage. A continuous back pressure will have to be applied to bring the aircraft out of the dive and back into a climb, after which, as the airspeed returns to the cruising figure, the throttle should be opened and the aircraft returned to cruising flight.

During your initial practice the primary objective will be to accomplish a smooth co-ordinated manoeuvre. Later on you will need to improve the accuracy of the loop in relation to entering and completing it on the same heading and following a symmetrical circular path throughout. In this last respect it should be appreciated that whereas loops can be satisfactorily performed from an initial pull up g of 2.5, a greater g force will have to be pulled on recovery if the loop is to describe a symmetrical circle. Therefore in the later stages of your practice you should aim to exit the loop with a g force of at least 3 to 3.5g.

FLIGHT EXERCISE

THE LOOP

(1) Safety checks completed and area cleared. Select a reference line feature. Final lookout. Commence the initial dive to obtain the entry airspeed and maintain balance whilst keeping the wings level.

(2) At the recommended airspeed, a firm pull back on the control column will be needed. Keep the wings level and the aircraft in balance.

(3) As the nose passes through the horizon re-check that the wings are level. As the speed decreases a progressive backward movement of the control column will be required. The direction of rudder pressure to maintain balance will change due to the change in yaw as the airspeed rapidly lowers.

(4) Use of a wing tip reference feature on the horizon can assist in the maintenance of direction at this stage.

(5) As the aircraft comes over the top of the loop, gentle pressures and control movements must be made because of the low airspeed.

(6) Look up and back to search for the horizon. Then check that the wings are laterally level.

(7) When the nose is below the horizon, reduce the power and ease off the back pressure to ensure a constant rate of pitch when pulling through the vertical. A change in rudder pressure to maintain balance should be anticipated at this stage.

(8) Re-identify the selected line feature and amend the aircraft's heading as necessary.

(9) Continue to pull through at a constant rate of pitch and ease from the dive into a climb. As the speed reduces gradually increase to cruising power and return to level flight.

GENERAL ADVICE
During the initial acceleration to achieve the entry airspeed a positive check should be made to ensure the wings are being kept level with the aircraft in balance.

The use of a wing tip reference feature on the horizon can assist in keeping the loop straight as the first quarter of the manoeuvre is reached.

To keep the pitch rate constant when the airspeed is reducing towards the end of the second quarter, it is essential to increase the rearward movement of the control column but this action must be carried out smoothly.

Upon passing through the inverted point the back pressure will need to be relaxed slightly to avoid producing an egg shaped figure.

With practice, the throttle may be used to smoothly maintain the RPM at a maximum permitted value (below the 'red line') dependent upon the changing airspeed.

If the loop is pulled too tight in the initial stages the increased angle of attack may lead to a stall. Recovery will be effected by relaxing the back pressure but this will probably result in arriving at the inverted position with little or no airspeed. If this occurs centralise the controls and wait for the nose to drop below the horizon. When the airspeed increases ease the aircraft out of the dive. It should however be appreciated that the same situation may result if the loop is entered too loosely.

Once you have achieved more proficiency at the loop, you should, after the entry speed has been attained, briefly establish level flight just prior to commencing the loop. You should also regain level flight momentarily at the end of the manoeuvre, as these refinements are a requirement for competition loops.

THE AILERON ROLL

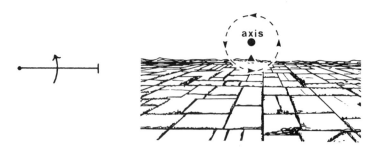

INTRODUCTION

Pure rolling manoeuvres can be divided into three types, these are the aileron roll, the barrel roll and the slow roll. Of these the aileron roll is easier to accomplish, primarily because the airspeed lowers less during the manoeuvre, thus the controls remain more effective throughout. It is therefore a more suitable rolling manoeuvre for the beginner to start with. In fact many instructors prefer to use this manoeuvre as an introduction to aerobatics.

Provided the aircraft is rolled at a suitably high rate there will be no negative g to contend with and this is a further advantage of using it as an introductory aerobatic manoeuvre. The maximum positive g force need not exceed more than 2 in the entry and exit, and you will have already acclimatised yourself to this during your pre-aerobatic training when practising steep turns at 60° of bank. Satisfactory performance of this manoeuvre will give a marked improvement to your confidence and co-ordination.

THE FLIGHT MANOEUVRE

This consists of a 360° roll about the longitudinal axis and is accomplished by using all three controls with the ailerons being considered as the primary control throughout. A reference point, well into the distance and preferably on or above the horizon line should be selected about which the line of the manoeuvre can be co-ordinated.

In the case of aircraft capable of higher speeds or those with a large rudder area, it will be possible to revolve the nose of the aircraft on the reference point. However most aircraft used in training are not capable of these higher speeds and many of them have a relatively small rudder area. Either of these limitations will therefore often make it impossible for the nose to be rotated on the reference point but a fairly tight orbit of the reference feature will nevertheless be possible.

Once the safety checks have been completed, and the area is ascertained as being clear of other aircraft, a reference feature should be selected and the aircraft placed in a shallow dive towards it. At the recommended entry speed the nose should be raised up to just above the reference point before commencing the roll. In the early stages of your practice it will be advisable to bring the nose up fairly high, to 30° above the horizon. This is a precaution against allowing the nose to drop too low during the final portion of the manoeuvre because of insufficient forward pressure being maintained on the control column during the inverted section.

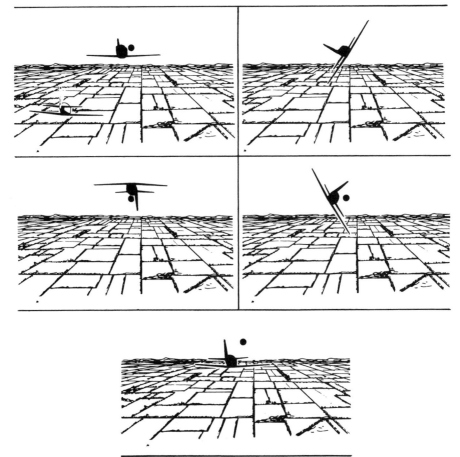

Fig. 28

The following comments relate to the various steps of the manoeuvre but it must be appreciated that in the practical sense the control movements assume a natural smooth flow. When the nose has been brought up to the correct position above the reference point a positive forward 'check' on the control column should be made before commencing the roll in the desired direction. The reason for this forward check is to reduce the tendency to continue the pull up as the roll is commenced and so produce a barrelling effect. To start the roll the ailerons should be used in a positive but smooth action together with the co-ordinated application of rudder. The airspeed will reduce progressively during the first half of the manoeuvre so aileron deflection will have to be progressively increased to maintain a constant rate of roll.

By the time the aircraft arrives in the inverted position it will be normal to have full aileron and rudder deflection and you will need to make a further conscious effort not to apply back pressure to the control column or the nose will be pulled down well below the horizon. When the aircraft approaches erect flight the controls should be centralised and the pitch attitude corrected to level flight.

During the roll the nose will be progressively dropping to around 30° below the horizon unless the elevators are used in the inverted section to sustain the selected reference point. This use of elevator may be considered a refinement to be introduced when you have gained confidence in the aileron roll.

The control actions mentioned in the previous paragraphs are listed in a relatively mechanical fashion, but in the actual performance of the manoeuvre it must be appreciated that the control deflection and the timing of your movements must be smooth and well co-ordinated.

FLIGHT EXERCISE

AILERON ROLL
(1) Safety checks completed and area cleared. Select a reference point. Final lookout.

(2) Commence the initial dive to obtain the entry airspeed, whilst keeping the wings level and the aircraft in balance.

(3) At the recommended airspeed raise the nose above the reference point in a positive manner. Following this, a brief check forward on the control column should be made to maintain the selected pitch attitude. Commence the roll by using aileron and rudder. As the airspeed decreases more deflection of the ailerons and rudder will be progressively required.

(4) By the time the aircraft reaches the inverted position full aileron and rudder will be needed to maintain the rate of roll. It will be essential not to apply any back pressure on the control column at this stage.

(5) During the roll from the inverted position to the three-quarter stage of the manoeuvre the ailerons and rudder will still have to be fully deflected.

(6) As the aircraft approaches the erect position all the controls are used in the normal manner to return the aircraft to straight and level flight.

GENERAL ADVICE

Be sure that you raise the nose to the correct position above the horizon during the initial stage. Failure to do so will cause the nose to drop too low through the inverted section.

Failure to maintain aileron and rudder deflection will lead to a slow rate of roll and will also cause the nose to drop too low, both of which will cause an unnecessary loss of altitude.

It will be necessary to neutralise the elevator action just prior to commencing the roll, or a barrelling effect will occur.

Failure to use sufficient rudder during the final stage of the roll will cause the aircraft to 'dish' out to one side.

If insufficient back pressure is applied during the last 45° of the roll, the nose will drop too low and cause a large loss in altitude.

THE BARREL ROLL

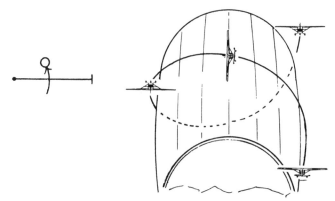

INTRODUCTION

This type of roll requires precise control co-ordination in order to prescribe a spiral path about the roll axis whilst keeping the aircraft in a balanced condition. Positive *g* is applied throughout the manoeuvre.

The name given to this manoeuvre is derived from the fact that when viewed from behind, the aircraft's path looks as though it were being flown around the outside of a barrel. This aerobatic is one in which a constant 'rolling pull' is applied throughout, but the control pressures will need to be altered with the variation in airspeed.

It is a comfortable and smooth manoeuvre to perform and will give you considerable satisfaction and additional confidence when you have learned to execute it properly.

THE FLIGHT MANOEUVRE

This consists of a 360° roll about a central axis which is displaced to one side of the aircraft. During the first half of the manoeuvre the aircraft will be rolling and climbing and in the second half it will be rolling and descending. However, back pressure on the control column will be required throughout, but it will not be necessary to pull more than approximately 2*g* at any time.

There are two ways of setting up the entry to a barrel roll. One is in which a reference point is selected about 30° off to one side of the aircraft's line of flight and slightly above the horizon. The aircraft is then gently dived to obtain the recommended entry speed following which a direct 'rolling pull up' is commenced to describe a circle about the chosen point.

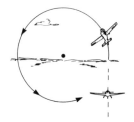

The other method of entry is to chose a reference point straight ahead and just above the horizon. A shallow dive is then commenced to obtain the entry speed during which the aircraft is turned about 30° to one side. After the correct speed has been obtained a 'rolling pull up' is commenced into the direction of the intended roll.

Either method may be used by your instructor but it will be of value to eventually learn and practise each method of entry. The following comments apply to the selection of a reference feature straight ahead of the aircraft, but with the exception of having to turn the aircraft slightly to one side during the initial dive, the control actions throughout the roll will be the same regardless of which entry method is used.

Once the safety checks have been completed select a reference feature and ensure that it is all clear around the aircraft and particularly ahead, above and below the intended manoeuvre area. In the early stages of your practice it will be advisable to use an axis line above the chosen ground feature which is being used as a reference point, or alternatively use a cloud just above the horizon as this will induce you to bring the nose fairly high as you pass through the top position, thus reducing the possibility of finishing up in a steep nose down spiral in the final stages of the manoeuvre.

For the purpose of the following comments, assume it is intended to carry out a barrel roll to the left. First, commence the shallow dive to obtain the recommended airspeed. As the correct airspeed is reached, start raising the nose up through the horizon and co-ordinate your control pressures so that the wings are maintained in the laterally level attitude. When the nose passes the point from which an aileron roll would be commenced, initiate a climbing roll to the left.

Figure 29 shows the progress of the manoeuvre as seen from behind. During Stage 2 the airspeed will still be relatively high and although a firm back pressure must be maintained the ailerons will still be very effective, thus only a small deflection will be required to maintain the rate of roll at a constant figure. As the aircraft approaches the highest point and proceeds into Stage 3 of the manoeuvre, the speed will be decreasing and the aileron deflection will have to be progressively increased to maintain a constant rate of roll.

As the aircraft reaches the inverted position at the end of Stage 3 the airspeed will be at its lowest and thus a slight relaxation of back pressure will be required. When the aircraft passes through the inverted position the nose will be coming down through the horizon and descending towards the bottom point of the manoeuvre where the

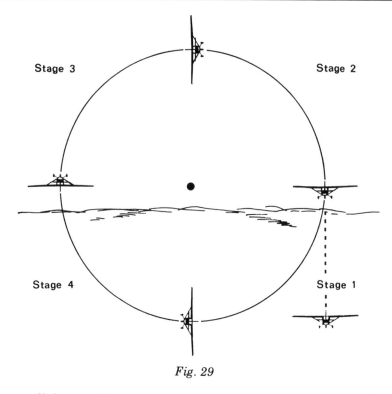

Stage 3   Stage 2

Stage 4   Stage 1

Fig. 29

wings will be at 90° to the horizontal. Thus the airspeed will be progressively increasing until the end of the roll. Aileron deflection will therefore have to be progressively decreased though a heavier back pressure on the control column will be required in this section, in order to keep a steady rate of 'pull through', until the wings are once again laterally level.

Throughout the whole manoeuvre rudder will be required in the normal sense to maintain the aircraft in balance, however, you will need to vary the rudder pressure to compensate for the changing airspeed. After initial practice the throttle can be used to assist in the accomplishment of the manoeuvre.

FLIGHT EXERCISE

BARREL ROLL

(1) Safety checks completed, area cleared and a reference feature selected about 30° off to the left. Final lookout. Commence the initial dive to obtain the entry airspeed.

(2) At the entry airspeed commence raising the nose up to the horizon and check that the wings are level.

(3) After the nose has passed through the horizon commence a climbing roll in the required direction. Strong back pressure and light aileron pressure will be required.

(4) At the highest point of the manoeuvre the wings should be passing through the 90° angle to the horizontal and directly above the reference point.

(5) During this stage the airspeed will be lowering and greater aileron deflection will be required to maintain a constant rate of roll. A slight relaxation of back pressure will be required.

(6) As the aircraft's nose reaches the horizon the aircraft should be in the inverted position with the wings passing through the level attitude.

(7) During this stage the nose will be descending and a strong back pressure will be required to maintain a constant rate of pull through. Aileron deflection should be adjusted to keep the roll rate constant.

(8) At the bottom point of the manoeuvre the wings will be at 90° to the horizontal and the aircraft's nose should be passing directly below the offset reference point.

(9) In the final stage the nose will be rising back to the horizon and the wings should be gradually returning to laterally level flight.

GENERAL ADVICE
The three most common errors are failure to bring the nose of the aircraft sufficiently high during the first half of the manoeuvre, failure to maintain sufficient back pressure, i.e. enough pull during the roll, and allowing the rate of roll to become too slow.

Any one or all of these errors will cause a very steep exit from the manoeuvre with a resulting high airspeed and unnecessary stress on the aircraft.

THE SLOW ROLL

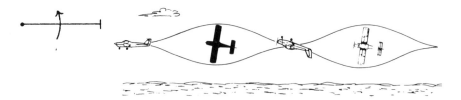

INTRODUCTION

Of the various types of roll this will be the most difficult to accomplish. The reason being the slow rate at which most aircraft can be rolled which leads to the airspeed dropping to a very low figure by the time the aircraft reaches the inverted position. This airspeed reduction is aggravated by the fact that most training aircraft are not equipped with fuel/oil systems which permit the engine to operate during the inverted flight phase. Therefore large control deflections and a positive change in rudder pressure in an abnormal sense are required beyond that used for normal flight. A further point is that due to the period spent in passing through the inverted position, negative g will occur and you will find your weight being transferred to the shoulder straps. Finally the aircraft will be in an unbalanced condition virtually throughout the manoeuvre, and this is necessary in order for the figure to be done correctly.

During your initial training in this manoeuvre you should start by rolling at a slightly slower rate than that which is used for an aileron roll.

THE FLIGHT MANOEUVRE

During the slow roll the aircraft is rotated round its longitudinal axis through 360° whilst in level flight. The rate at which it is rolled will depend upon the entry speed, the position of the nose above the horizon from which the roll is started and the degree of aileron deflection being used at any time during the manoeuvre.

During a really slow roll it will not be possible (unless engine power is available) to actually rotate the nose on the reference point, but instead the nose will prescribe an orbital path around the reference feature or selected axis point. Having said this you should nevertheless attempt to hold the nose on the reference point throughout the manoeuvre, as failure to do so will cause the nose to increase its radius from the reference axis. One small but important consideration in this respect, is that for any given airspeed the lift generated by the wings at a particular angle of attack will be less when the wings are inverted. Thus, to reduce altitude loss when in the inverted stage of the aerobatic it will be necessary to have a higher angle of attack, i.e. the nose will have to be higher in relation to the horizon.

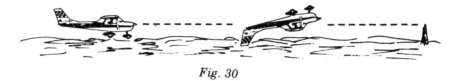

Fig. 30

One way of learning how to accomplish a slow roll is to consider the manoeuvre in two halves. The first half is that section from the entry to the inverted position and the second half is that section from the inverted position to the end of the figure.

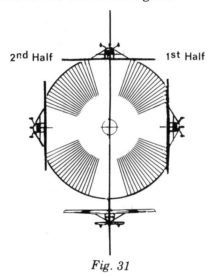

Fig. 31

Your instructor will have developed his own teaching technique in relation to the slow roll and he will use this to your advantage. However because of the differences between the actual methods used by instructors when first teaching the manoeuvre the following comments will be confined to the way the slow roll is actually executed.

Once the safety checks have been completed and you have ensured that the area is clear of other aircraft, a reference feature should be selected and an imaginary axis point, at least 20° above the horizon should be used as the rotation point. A shallow dive will normally be necessary to obtain the recommended entry speed, following which the nose of the aircraft is raised to the rotation point. When the nose reaches this point a firm and positive forward check should be made to the control column to avoid barrelling and the roll commenced in the required direction. The ailerons will be used to commence the roll and the other controls should be used to prevent the aircraft from turning away from its heading. The following applies to a slow roll to the left.

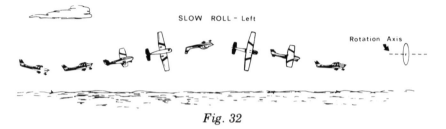

SLOW ROLL - Left

Rotation Axis

Fig. 32

As the wings approach the vertical there will be a tendency for the nose to drop and in this vertical attitude any fore or aft movement of the control column will only take the nose away from the reference point, so a little right (top) rudder will be required to retard the downward movement of the nose. The amount of rudder required for this purpose will depend upon the airspeed, roll rate, and the nose position above the horizon from which the roll was commenced. Therefore the correct pressure which will be needed can only be determined when carrying out the individual manoeuvre.

As the aircraft approaches the inverted position, the effect of the rudder in reducing the tendency for the nose to drop will diminish, and the elevators will now have to be used to keep the nose up in the correct position. Consequently at this stage a positive forward pressure on the control column will be required.

The adverse yaw experienced whenever an aircraft is rolled will be such, that as the aircraft continues rolling through the inverted stage into the second half of the roll, the nose will tend to yaw to the left when the roll is to the left. Therefore some of the right rudder applied during the first half will still be needed to prevent the aircraft's nose being pulled away to the left of the rotation point. An appreciation of this effect is given in the following paragraph.

Whenever an aircraft is rolled about the longitudinal axis an adverse yaw action will occur. This is because the lift acting at 90° to the relative airflow will be tilted slightly forward on the downgoing wing and slightly backwards on the upgoing wing as shown in Fig. 33. The result of these tilted lift lines is to effectively produce more drag on the upgoing wing and less on the downgoing wing. Thus a yawing moment will be introduced relative to the line of flight and cause the aircraft to tend to yaw to the right whenever it is being rolled to the left and vice versa.

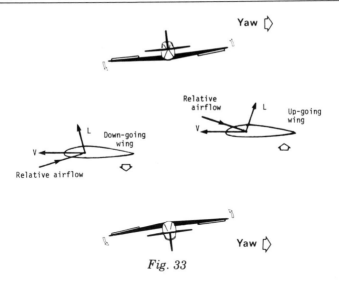

Fig. 33

Having entered the second half of the roll the rudder pressure will initially need to be relaxed and upon approaching the 270° stage of the roll, opposite rudder (in this case left rudder) will be needed to resist the tendency for the nose to drop as the wings pass the vertical and through into the final stage. An additional point to remember is that following the inverted period the speed will be very low until the final quarter of the roll where it will be increasing again. Therefore a fairly large left rudder deflection will be required to prevent the nose dropping as you pass through the 270° position. This left rudder will tend to increase the rate of roll (further effect of rudder) so this will have to be counteracted by a reduction in aileron deflection.

Throughout the second stage of the slow roll the forward pressure being applied to the control column will have to be gradually relaxed and then converted to a back pressure which will need to be fairly strong during the last 45° of the manoeuvre.

Finally, it should be appreciated that as the manoeuvre is completed the aircraft will be in a crossed control condition which will need to be corrected before the aircraft is being returned to normal straight and level flight.

FLIGHT EXERCISE

SLOW ROLL

(1) Safety checks completed and area cleared. Select a reference feature. Final lookout. Commence the initial dive to obtain the entry airspeed.

(2) At the recommended airspeed raise the nose to the rotation point

(at least 20° above the horizon). Make a positive check forward on the control column.

(3) Commence the roll in the required direction through the use of aileron and rudder. Control the rate of roll with the ailerons.

(4) Maintain the rate of roll by use of the ailerons and use the other controls to keep the nose of the aircraft on the reference point. Use top rudder in a progressive fashion to prevent the nose from dropping below the reference axis.

(5) Move the control column progressively forward to maintain the nose position as the aircraft rolls into the semi inverted attitude. Maintain application of rudder to prevent adverse yaw as the aircraft rolls through the inverted position and continue to apply forward pressure on the control column to keep the nose from dropping below the reference axis.

(6) On entering the second half of the roll the rudder pressure can be relaxed. Following which opposite rudder (top rudder) will be needed to prevent the nose from dropping below the reference axis. When applying opposite rudder the aileron deflection will need to be decreased to prevent an increase in the rate of roll. The forward pressure on the control column can be gradually relaxed on approaching the 270° position in roll.

(7) In the final quarter of the roll back pressure will need to be applied to maintain the nose position in relation to the rotation point.

(8) As the aircraft returns to straight and level flight the crossed control condition should be corrected and a co-ordinated use of all the three controls will be necessary to establish the normal level flight attitude.

GENERAL ADVICE

Prior to commencing this manoeuvre it is important to ensure that your harness is extremely tight and you should bear in mind that because of the negative g associated with this aerobatic figure, any loose cockpit items (including loose dirt, mud particles, etc.), will come adrift during the inverted section. Therefore any loose items should be firmly stowed and the cockpit floor should be as clean as possible.

Common faults will include failure to move the control column sufficiently far forward during the inverted section, failure to close the throttle when inverted, and not using sufficient rudder at the 270°

point in the second half of the roll.

During training there will also be a tendency for you to forget to harmonise the rate and amount of aileron deflection in order to maintain a constant rate of roll, particularly when passing through the inverted section of the manoeuvre.

THE STALL TURN

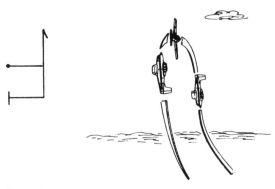

INTRODUCTION

This is probably the most difficult of the basic aerobatic manoeuvres to perform and calls for very precise timing, orientation, and co-ordination of control movements.

It is also an extremely valuable one to practise as it will improve your ability to cope with the recovery from situations in which the aircraft has been pulled up into the vertical or near vertical attitude, and where the airspeed has been allowed to drop so low that proper control over the aircraft cannot be retained.

THE FLIGHT MANOEUVRE

This consists of bringing the aircraft up to a vertical attitude and then using the rudder to yaw through 180° about the normal axis so that the aircraft is facing in the opposite direction to that of the entry. In effect the aircraft is cartwheeled sideways from a vertical climb until it is pointing vertically downwards, following which it is eased out of the dive and returned to level flight.

In aircraft which are equipped with a propeller which rotates clockwise (as in American built engines) the propeller rotation, torque, and slipstream effects, will produce a positive yaw to the left when the aircraft is flown in the lower speed range. Because of this effect therefore, it will be easier to perform stall turns to the left in these aircraft.

Once the safety checks have been completed and you have ensured the area is clear of other aircraft you should choose a reference line and align the aircraft along it. It will also be helpful to select a reference point on the horizon at 90° to the reference line and on the same side as the direction of the intended stall turn. This second reference feature can then be used as a guide which will enable you to maintain the reference track after the nose has been raised and when

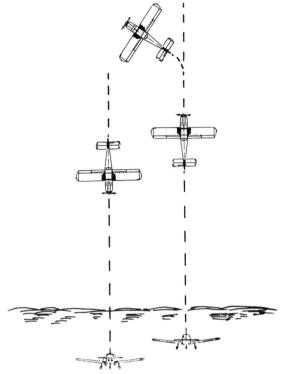

Fig. 34

the reference line feature is no longer visible to you.

Complete a final lookout and commence a shallow dive along the reference line to obtain the required entry speed. Once the recommended airspeed has been attained a firm and positive 'pull up' towards the vertical should be made. Aileron and rudder will be required to keep the wings laterally level and the aircraft in balance. Once established in the climb full power should be applied and the lookout transferred to the 90° reference feature.

Although the ideal will be to have the aircraft in a precisely vertical attitude at the time rudder is applied to cartwheel (in this case to the left), it will be advisable in the early stage of training to check forward on the control column when just short of the vertical. This will reduce the possibility of pulling the aircraft past the vertical and spoiling the manoeuvre by getting into a partially inverted attitude during the cartwheel stage.

As the aircraft approaches the vertical the airspeed will have become very low and positive rudder pressure will be necessary to maintain a balanced condition, and aileron may be required to maintain the wing tip on the 90° reference point.

Assuming the stall turn is intended to be to the left, once the

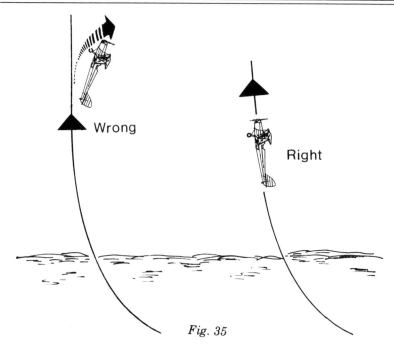

Wrong

Right

Fig. 35

aircraft is established in the required vertical attitude, full left rudder should be applied and as the nose comes down towards the 90° reference point the throttle should be closed. At this stage forward pressure on the control column will still be needed and the ailerons must be used as required to prevent rolling. Thus all three controls are used to fly the aircraft from the vertical to the point where the nose cuts through the horizon at the 90° reference point.

As the nose approaches the vertical diving attitude, opposite rudder (in this case right rudder) should be used to stop the downward swing passing through the true vertical position and the control column can be used to prevent any tendency to 'tuck under'. In effect, during this stage, all three controls will be used in the natural sense to point the aircraft straight down with its wings laterally level.

Within a second or two of achieving the correct vertical attitude, back pressure should be firmly applied whilst the airspeed is relatively low. The aircraft is then smoothly eased out of the dive and after the nose has come up above the horizon, power is re-applied and the aircraft returned to level flight.

Stall turns in the direction opposite to the yaw produced by the propeller will require the following modification to the technique used during the cartwheel stage of the manoeuvre.

From the vertical attitude and after the application of rudder the rate of yaw will become fairly critical; at first the yaw will be quite strong, then due to the natural effect of slipstream whilst using full power, the yaw produced by the rudder action will weaken. Therefore as the rate of yaw slows down it will be necessary to slowly reduce the power whilst increasing the rudder deflection to the maximum. It will be very important to co-ordinate the increase in rudder deflection with the reduction in power to prevent the yaw from stopping or the initial sideways momentum produced by the rudder will be lost. This action will prevent the cartwheel action from being sufficiently effective and the aircraft will fall out of the manoeuvre.

FLIGHT EXERCISE

STALL TURN TO THE LEFT

(1) Safety checks completed and area cleared. Select a reference line feature and a 90° reference point. Final lookout. Commence the initial dive.

(2) At the recommended airspeed apply back pressure on the control column to bring the aircraft up into a vertical climbing attitude. Keep the wings level and maintain balance. As the nose rises above the horizon apply full throttle.

(3) Just before the vertical attitude is reached apply a positive forward pressure to the control column to check the aircraft in the vertical attitude.

(4) Lookout to the left as the aircraft approaches the vertical and use the 90° reference point to maintain the line of the manoeuvre. Use aileron and rudder as required to keep the wings aligned with the lateral axis and to maintain balanced flight.

(5) Use sufficient forward pressure on the control column to maintain the vertical position and apply left rudder to cartwheel the aircraft to the left. Opposite aileron will be required to prevent any movement in roll. As the nose comes down towards the 90° reference point close the throttle smoothly and use the elevators to ensure the nose passes through the 90° reference point.

(6) As the nose drops down towards the vertical commence to apply opposite rudder to check the swing and ensure the aircraft points straight down. A slight back pressure on the control column may be necessary at this stage.

(7) When the vertical attitude has been achieved commence to increase back pressure in a positive manner to rotate the nose in the pitching plane and raise it up towards the horizon. As the nose passes

through the horizon gradually increase the power and return to level flight.

GENERAL ADVICE

If you do not make a sufficiently firm forward check on the control column at the vertical position before the application of rudder, it will not be possible to perform a good manoeuvre.

At the point where rudder is applied to cartwheel the aircraft airspeed is critical and if rudder is applied at too low or too high an airspeed a poorly executed manoeuvre will result. Although it will not be easy during your initial practice to note the airspeed whilst looking at the 90° reference point, a check of the airspeed should be introduced as soon as possible into your practice.

Finally, be careful not to pull out of the manoeuvre until the aircraft is pointing vertically downwards.

HALF CUBAN 8

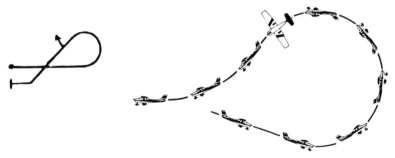

INTRODUCTION

This is a combination manoeuvre commencing with a normal loop which is then converted into a half aileron roll, thus bringing the aircraft out of the manoeuvre on a reciprocal heading to that of entry.

The timing of the half roll should be such that when the aircraft has completed ⅝ of a loop and is approaching the 45° nose down inverted attitude, the half roll is commenced, bringing the aircraft into the normal erect position from which it is returned to level flight.

You will need to have reached a good standard of competence in looping and rolling manoeuvres before this manoeuvre can be satisfactorily performed.

THE FLIGHT MANOEUVRE

Select a suitable line feature, preferably into or down wind and position the aircraft over or parallel to it. During this positioning phase you should complete the safety checks and ensure that the area is clear of other aircraft.

A shallow dive will usually be necessary to obtain the entry speed. The manoeuvre can normally be commenced at the recommended entry speed for a loop, but some manuals may quote a higher speed.

Once the entry speed has been obtained, enter a normal loop and maintain the looping phase until the aircraft has passed over the top. Ideally the roll should be commenced when the aircraft is approaching the 45° nose down inverted attitude, i.e. approximately ⅝ of the way through the loop. At this point a forward pressure on the control column will be required to stop the loop. The ailerons should then be used to roll the aircraft through a diving half roll on the 45° axis.

At this stage the airspeed will not need to be as high as when performing a horizontal aileron roll because the nose will be pointing down at 45° to the horizon and therefore the speed will be continuously increasing throughout the rolling section of the manoeuvre. During the rolling period it should be remembered that the

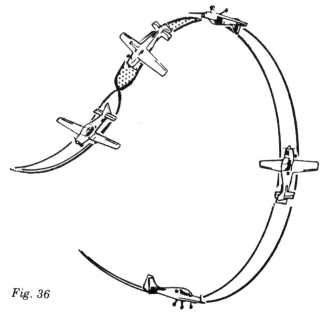

Fig. 36

aircraft will want to turn away from the reference line, particularly as the wings approach the vertical. Your control inputs will therefore need to be similar to those used in a normal roll. During the roll the throttle should be retarded to avoid exceeding the limiting RPM. Upon completion of the roll the aircraft's nose should still be pointing down at an angle of 45° and at this stage the nose of the aircraft should be firmly but smoothly brought up to the horizon and level flight re-established.

FLIGHT EXERCISE

HALF CUBAN
(1) Safety checks completed and area cleared. Select a reference line feature. Position the aircraft and have a final lookout. The manoeuvre is started with the commencement of a normal loop.

(2) Ensure the reference line is maintained throughout the looping section.

(3) As the 45° nose down inverted position is approached, apply forward pressure on the control column and commence the roll, retarding the throttle as necessary.

(4) Continue the roll to the erect position whilst maintaining the reference line at a 45° downward angle.

(5) When the roll is completed, ease the aircraft up into the level flight attitude.

GENERAL ADVICE

Before tackling this manoeuvre you will already have achieved a degree of competence in loops and rolls, therefore the advice contained under this heading can be reduced to the actions taken in converting from the looping section to the aileron roll. The most common error at this point is in the timing of the change from the loop to the roll and here you will have to be careful to avoid the tendency of initiating the roll at too late a stage in the manoeuvre. Commencing the roll too late will inevitably result in an excessive airspeed leading to unnecessarily high g forces during the return to erect level flight.

REVERSE HALF CUBAN 8

INTRODUCTION

Once the half Cuban 8 has been mastered an interesting variation to practise will be to reverse the order of the loop and roll. In the reverse Cuban manoeuvre the aircraft is initially brought up into a 45° climbing attitude, then half rolled to the inverted position from which the second half of a loop can be accomplished.

Practice at this manoeuvre will further develop your sense of timing and your co-ordination and orientation.

THE FLIGHT MANOEUVRE

First, select a line feature and once again it will be preferable to choose one either upwind or downwind. Next complete the safety checks and ensure the area is clear of other aircraft whilst positioning along the chosen reference line.

A shallow dive will normally be necessary to obtain the recommended entry speed. If the aircraft manual does not quote a speed for this manoeuvre your instructor will inform you of the best speed to use for the aircraft type. This speed will usually be less than the entry speed for the half Cuban 8 in order to ensure that the looping section is commenced from a very low speed, thus preventing an excessive build up of airspeed during the pull through from the loop.

Once the entry speed is achieved a fairly brisk rotation should be made to raise the nose into the 45° climbing attitude, and as the airspeed starts to decrease the throttle should be opened to the full power position. The aircraft should be momentarily held in the 45° position and then a half roll can be commenced in the desired direction.

Once the aircraft reaches the inverted attitude, pause briefly whilst maintaining forward pressure on the control column and check that the wings are laterally level. This momentary pause will help to ensure the airspeed has dropped to a very low figure before the

Fig. 37

commencement of the looping phase. Following this the second half of a normal loop can be commenced but care must be taken to make a positive backward movement of the control column in order to pull the aircraft through the vertical before the speed becomes excessive. Any delay in this action, once the nose has dropped below the horizontal, will allow the speed to increase rapidly, and very strong control force will be needed to bring the aircraft out of the loop before the V_{ne} is reached. The throttle should be retarded as necessary to remain below the limiting RPM.

The final stage of the manoeuvre consists of completing the loop and returning the aircraft to the normal erect level flight attitude.

FLIGHT EXERCISE

REVERSE HALF CUBAN
(1) Safety checks completed and area cleared. Select a reference line feature. Position the aircraft and have a final lookout. Commence a shallow dive to obtain the entry airspeed, whilst maintaining the reference line and keeping the wings level.

(2) Briskly raise the nose to the 45° climbing attitude whilst opening the throttle fully.

(3) Pause momentarily and then commence a half roll in the required direction.

(4) Once in the inverted position, pause briefly maintaining forward pressure on the control column and checking that the wings are laterally level before starting the looping section.

(5) Commence the pull through into the second half of a loop. Initially a positive back pressure should be applied to bring the aircraft through the vertical before excessive speed builds up. The throttle should be retarded as necessary to remain below the limiting RPM.

(6) Continue the loop until the aircraft is in the normal erect level flight attitude.

GENERAL ADVICE

As with the half Cuban 8 the main advice which can be given under this heading concerns the change from the half roll to the half loop and in this case it can be confined to emphasising the need for the aircraft to be brought up to at least the 45° climbing attitude, before the half loop is commenced. Failure to get the aircraft's nose sufficiently high before commencing the half loop will automatically lead to an excessively high airspeed during the final stage of the manoeuvre.

ROLL OFF THE TOP OF A LOOP

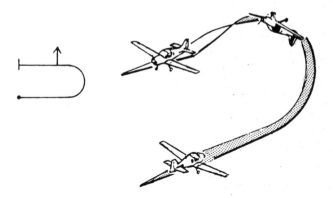

INTRODUCTION

This manoeuvre consists of the first half of a loop and the second half of a roll which will bring the aircraft from the inverted section of a loop into the erect level flight attitude.

Due to the need to maintain the best possible aileron effectiveness throughout the period of roll, it will be necessary to use a higher entry speed than for the loop or the half Cuban 8. The manoeuvre will effect a 180° change of aircraft direction and a gain in altitude from the point of entry.

In execution it is similar to a half Cuban 8 but differs in respect of the point at which the rolling section is commenced, i.e. in the roll off the top, the roll is started before the nose comes down below the horizon line and is commenced when the nose is approximately 30° above the horizon.

THE FLIGHT MANOEUVRE

Select a suitable line feature, preferably into or downwind and position the aircraft over or parallel to it. During this positioning phase you should complete the safety checks and ensure the area is clear of other aircraft.

A shallow dive will usually be necessary to obtain the recommended entry airspeed which will be about 15 to 20 knots higher than that used for the basic loop. Once the entry speed has been obtained a positive 'pull up' should be initiated and the throttle will need to be opened to the maximum position. During this increase in power care should be taken not to exceed the limiting RPM. A fairly tight looping section must be achieved and maintained (about 3.5 g) to ensure that the airspeed at the top of the loop is still sufficient to allow good aileron effectiveness for the rolling section.

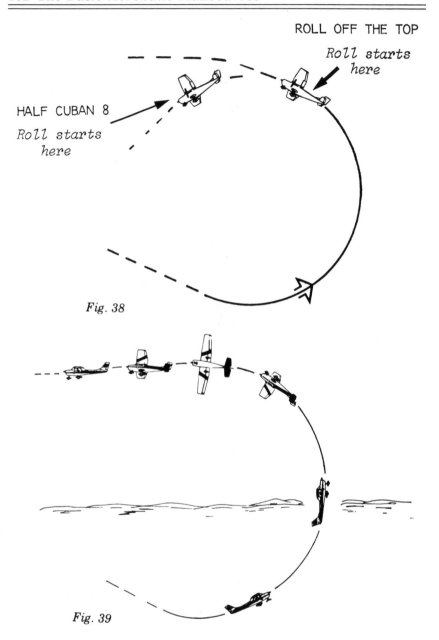

ROLL OFF THE TOP

Roll starts here

HALF CUBAN 8

Roll starts here

Fig. 38

Fig. 39

As the aircraft approaches the inverted attitude, incline your head backwards and look for the horizon. When the nose is approximately 30° above the horizon a positive forward pressure should be applied to the control column in order to arrest the loop. Pause momentarily and then commence the rolling to the left or right as desired.

Although you will be using an entry speed which is significantly higher than that used for a loop, the airspeed during the rolling section will inevitably be very low and full aileron deflection will be required to maintain the rate of roll which at best will be rather slow. Throughout the rolling stage the controls should be used in the same manner as for the second half of a slow roll, and it is important to bear in mind that a positive forward pressure on the control column will have to be maintained or the nose will drop below the horizon, thus causing the manoeuvre to terminate in a shallow dive instead of in the level flight attitude.

Another point to remember is that the direction of propeller rotation with its tendency to create a strong yawing action at high power and low airspeed, will have a significant effect upon the performance of the manoeuvre. If the propeller rotation is clockwise (when viewed from the cockpit), you will find it easier to accomplish rolls to the left, so it will be a good idea to use this direction of roll during your initial practice and then when a reasonable standard of competence has been achieved you should extend your efforts to achieving the same standard whilst rolling to the right.

FLIGHT EXERCISE

ROLL OFF THE TOP

(1) Safety checks completed and area cleared. Select a line feature and position the aircraft. Final lookout. Dive to obtain entry speed.

(2) Initiate and maintain a tight looping manoeuvre whilst smoothly opening the throttle to maximum power.

(3) After passing through the vertical, search for the horizon line. When the nose is approximately 30° above the horizon apply a positive forward pressure to the control column.

(4) Pause momentarily and then commence a positive roll in the desired direction. Large aileron deflection will be required and must be accomplished smoothly.

(5) Gradually reduce power and continue to apply control inputs as for the second half of a slow roll.

(6) The manoeuvre should be completed with the aircraft in the erect level flight attitude and at cruise power.

GENERAL ADVICE

The first part of the loop must be fairly tight in order to ensure that sufficient airspeed is available for the roll out at the top of the figure. The time to start the half roll from the top of the loop can be compared to the position of the aircraft nose when inverted during a slow roll.

Two fairly common faults during the roll section are to use insufficient top rudder, and failure to close the throttle whilst rolling through the inverted section.

THE SNAP ROLL

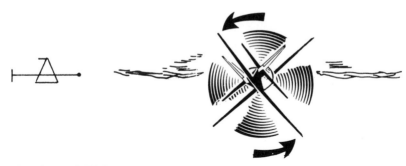

INTRODUCTION

This manoeuvre (also known as the 'flick roll') is one in which the aeroplane moves in all three planes. It is in effect a state of induced autorotation from a dynamic stall.

A one turn snap roll is a manoeuvre which lasts about three to four seconds from start to finish, depending upon the aircraft type and speed of entry. Due to this short time factor, the movement of the controls and the timing of these movements will be critical to the accomplishment of a clean recovery to level flight. You will therefore need plenty of practice to become accustomed to the rapid rate of roll and to develop the ability to recover in a wings level attitude.

Due to the potential stress, which could be imposed upon the aeroplane if the manoeuvre is entered at too high an airspeed, it will be extremely important not to exceed the recommended entry speed.

The following description of how the manoeuvre is accomplished will, in general apply to most aircraft, but there will be slight differences in the amount and timing of control movements and the use of power between different aircraft. Bearing in mind your own degree of experience and ability, you may find slight variations in procedure can be used to achieve a cleaner entry and in any case your instructor will advise you in this respect.

THE FLIGHT MANOEUVRE

Select a suitable feature near to or on the horizon line so that you can measure the degree of straightness achieved in the manoeuvre. Following this, complete the safety checks and determine that the area is clear of other aircraft. Select the power recommended in the aircraft manual, and at this stage it will normally be necessary to raise the nose to achieve the correct entry speed.

Note: Most training aircraft will have a recommended entry speed which is lower than the 'Manoeuvre Speed'. This will usually mean that the manoeuvre will have to be started with the aircraft in a nose high attitude, about 15° above the horizon. This pitch attitude will be helpful during your early practice because it will reduce any tendency for the nose to drop too low during the recovery stage.

Fig. 40

At, or just below the recommended entry speed, (never above) positively apply full rudder in the required direction of roll and at the same time move the control column backwards to its rearmost position. At this stage it must be stressed that a firm and positive movement of the controls must be made, leading very slightly with the rudder and ensuring that the control column is moved backwards in one continuous movement to its fully aft position. Any hesitation will spoil the entry and will most likely lead to a spin. The correct actions will lead to an extremely rapid rate of roll, however some aircraft may perform the manoeuvre better if the ailerons are used to assist, due to the degree of washout built into some wing designs. In any event this fact will normally be covered by the instructions given in the aircraft manual for the particular type of aircraft.

Recovery is effected by applying full opposite rudder to the direction of roll and moving the control column forward in a positive manner until the aircraft is unstalled. At this point the roll will stop, and all three controls can be used the normal way to re-establish straight and level flight.

The exact time to initiate recovery so that on completion the wings are level will depend upon the aircraft type and the rate at which the controls are moved, but in general the time to take recovery action will be after the aircraft has passed the inverted position and when about three-quarters of the roll has been accomplished. A further consideration in the timing of the recovery actions will concern the direction of roll relative to the direction of propeller rotation. This is because power is used throughout the manoeuvre, and the effect of the yaw produced by the propeller rotation at low airspeed will cause a faster rate of roll in one direction and a slower rate of roll in the other. If the propeller rotates in a clockwise direction as viewed from the cockpit, the faster rate of roll will occur when rolling left.

FLIGHT EXERCISE

SNAP ROLL
(1) Select a reference point on or near the horizon line. Complete the safety checks and ensure that no other aircraft are in the vicinity.

(2) Select the recommended power and raise the nose as necessary to obtain the correct entry speed.

(3) When the recommended entry speed is achieved sharply apply full rudder in the required direction and bring the control column back to its limit.

(4) When the aircraft has rolled through approximately 270°, apply full opposite rudder and move the control column sharply forward to break the stall. At this stage the rotation will cease.

(5) Use all three controls to adjust the flight attitude for straight and level flight.

GENERAL ADVICE
The most common problems encountered in commencing this manoeuvre are as follows:

> Not moving the control column back far enough or fast enough at the point of entry, thereby causing more of a 'mush' than a snap.
> Not using full rudder at the point of entry, and/or using aileron to start the rolling action.

The timing of the use of elevators and rudder during the recovery will be critical, and a fair amount of practice will be required to perfect the exit into the straight and level flight attitude.

Both the timing and amount of forward control column movement and opposite rudder application will depend upon the type of aircraft.

Combinations of aerobatic manoeuvres

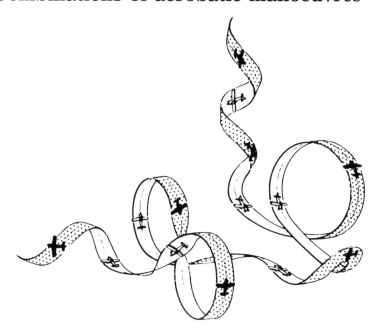

SUMMARY

You will already have practised certain manoeuvres in which sections of rolling and looping were combined. For example, the half Cuban 8 which starts with an entry to a loop and finishes with one half of a roll. Once the basic aerobatic manoeuvres have been mastered and a reasonable standard of proficiency has been attained, you will be ready to advance to manoeuvres carried out in immediate sequence with one another.

These sequences can be of varying length but it will be advisable to limit your early practice to just two aerobatic manoeuvres carried out in sequence and then as proficiency improves you can extend the number of aerobatic manoeuvres contained in the sequence. When carrying out a sequence of any length there are three important airmanship considerations to keep in mind. One is the question of your height above the surface. It will often be easy to get carried away and not notice when the aircraft has descended below a minimum safe altitude.

The second consideration relates to the need for maintaining an extremely good lookout during the whole sequence. Remember that many aeroplanes travel at cruising speeds which could bring them into your cleared area within a very short time (measured in seconds) after your initial lookout was made.

Finally there remains the constant need to maintain your orientation in relation to the aircraft's position over the surface. Throughout any sequence the aircraft will be affected by the wind and at the altitudes where you might be practising your sequences, the wind strength could often be in the region of 50 knots and so it will be important to plan your sequence headings with this in mind. Failure to do this may mean the aircraft could drift into the vicinity of aerodrome traffic patterns, controlled airspace, danger areas, etc.

In the case of competition aerobatics the sequence design should be aimed at conserving energy whilst maintaining an interesting mix of looping, rolling, yawed and stalled manoeuvres. Energy conservation is best obtained by ensuring that the exit airspeed from a preceding manoeuvre is the same as the entry airspeed for the next. The sequence design must also take into account the effects of wind in relation to maintaining the aircraft position within the aerobatic box. As you progress with your practice in competition sequences you should make use of both axes of the box by means of quarter vertical rolls, up or down, or alternatively use the $\frac{3}{4}$ or $1\frac{1}{4}$ turn spin to alter the axis of your manoeuvre.

Your instructor will advise you on the types of sequences which can be undertaken at your level of experience and proficiency. On those occasions when you are operating on your own however, you will need to take positive steps to ensure that the planned sequence includes only those manoeuvres which are permitted for the aircraft type. It will also be your own responsibility to ensure that the aircraft's weight and centre of gravity are within the limits for the aerobatic manoeuvres which are to be performed.

One final word: should you ever exceed the g limitations or V_{ne} of the aircraft you must be honest with yourself and others and report the occurrence immediately after landing and have the aircraft inspected by a qualified aircraft engineer.

In conclusion, we hope that you have enjoyed your introduction to aerobatic flight and remind you that should you wish to proceed to a more advanced stage or participate in competition aerobatic events we advise you to join the British Aerobatic Association and so give yourself the opportunity of receiving the best possible advice for your future proficiency and pleasure in this sport.

Index